From BRISBANE to KARACHI

KARACHI

with the Test Match Special team

Edited by Peter Baxter

Macdonald
Queen Anne Press

Frontispiece: *Imran Khan – ten wickets at Headingley to lead Pakistan to victory*
All-Sport/Adrian Murrell

A *Queen Anne Press* Book

© Queen Anne Press 1988
Scoresheets copyright © Bill Frindall

First published in Great Britain 1988 by
Queen Anne Press, a division of
Macdonald & Co (Publishers) Ltd
3rd Floor
Greater London House
Hampstead Road
London
NW1 7QX
A member of Maxwell Pergamon Publishing
Corporation plc

Jacket picture and illustrations by Paul Russell

British Library Cataloguing in Publication Data
From Brisbane to Karachi.
1. Test matches (Cricket) — England —
History
I. Baxter, Peter, *1947* –
796.35'865   GV928.G7

ISBN 0-356-15584-6

Typeset by York House Typographic Ltd, London
Reproduced, printed and bound in Great Britain
by Purnell Book Production Ltd, a member of BPCC plc, Paulton

Contents

Foreword (Defensive)

Willie Rushton

I never did discover where London Weekend Television heard the foul rumour that *Test Match Special* was due for the chop, but anyway as a Visually Exciting Person with a known Love for the Game, I was summoned to the top floor of the pavilion at Lord's to vent spleen. I realised that there was little point in saying anything that lasted longer than 30 seconds as it was one of those programmes that worries over-much about its audience's attention-span. So I sat on this rain-soaked bench and played it pretty tight, which is what Middlesex and Essex were doing downstairs. Blofeld has just done 17 minutes of pretty flash stuff. He'd be lucky to be on for a minute. 17 for one, then, and I'm in. The occasional one-liner past mid-wicket, a lucky quip through the slips, it was going quite well. I remember one mildly elaborate shot through the covers about My Perfect Summer's Day – listening to *Test Match Special*, I said, Pimms in hand, wearing old red-and-yellow blazer and boater, bees buzzing, mowers whirring, lolling the while on, say, Tina Turner.

6

Then after about ten minutes, nine of which at least were destined for the cutting-room floor, there was a query about the Englishness of it all, and a thought occurred to me that has never occurred to me previously, and it struck me as so true and so à propos that I remember thinking 'Sod their brief attention span! Cop this!' and launching into a peroration that ran roughly thus. Straight from the heart.

'Unlike the other peoples that form the United Kingdom, the English are alone in having no recognisably national costume, song or dance. The Scots have their kilts, their cabers, they blow bagpipes and dance in the Highland manner. The Welsh have eisteddfods, Druids, fly-halves and bushy eyebrows. The Irish have more of all that sort of stuff than is good for them. But the English have no . . . I lie!' I cried, startling myself and causing the sound-man to scream soundlessly. 'Yes, by God, we have! Cricket is our national dance, and *Test Match Special* is the music we dance to.'

Hold the *Oxford Book of Quotations*! Get the Job Centre to send me a Boswell! Be fair, that wasn't bad on the spur of the moment.

I said it came from the heart. It does. Let the names of Johnston, Trueman, Bailey, Blofeld, Martin-Jenkins, Mosey and Frindall be squeezed from the icing-bag in letters 22 yards high on top of the largest seed-cake ever created by a nice old lady from Croydon!

Love

Willie Rushton

P.S. Since writing the above there has been the hoo-ha in Faisalabad and talk of the very World War that Reagan and Gorbachev were seeking to avoid at that very moment. Cricket will survive it, believe me, Honest Will, the man who said Australia would take the World Cup. If you don't believe me, turn to Radio 3 next summer and listen to the voices of Sweet Reason. There you are, you see. Lie back and think of England.

England in Australia 1986-87

Peter Baxter, Christopher Martin—Jenkins, Jack Bannister

Thursday 9 October, London A tingling sense of excitement and anticipation is ever present on the departure day of a cricket tour. The old hands who have seen it all before try to look as if it is all in a day's work, but it is the beginning of term: reunion with friends; farewell to family; departure for unknown trials ahead. TCCB officials, sponsors and agents mingle with photographers, television news crews and reporters. Usually the players are accompanied on their outward flight by some ten journalists; a hard core which will be added to when the Test matches start. This time it was noticeable how few of my colleagues were taking the flight. The season at home finished only three weeks ago and four and a half months stretch ahead.

I broke into an end-of-season holiday to put the finishing touches to the administration which always precedes the broadcasting of a major tour, culminating in an 80-page schedule of reports and commentaries on all the domestic radio networks, the World Service and even breakfast television. The players have barely had any time for a break and the senior ones have already played three Test series – 11 Tests – in 1986. It cannot have helped tired limbs that eight of them ended in defeat and none of them in victory.

Still, the management seem in genial but firm control. 'No interviews except with manager, captain or cricket manager', said Peter Lush, usually the TCCB's marketing executive, but for this tour the England team manager. So I was soon settled into a deep leather sofa interviewing Micky Stewart, whose appointment as cricket manager is such an important development for this tour and the future. Around us players mouthed greetings, signed autograph sheets and bats and tried on the new blazers. In a far corner a tailor was sewing away rather self-consciously. Ian Botham's trousers, it seemed, needed letting out.

P.B.

The first few days of the tour were to be covered for BBC Radio, principally the Radio 2 Sports Desks, by Peter West, whose appointment as tour correspondent for the Daily Telegraph *had surprised almost everyone (including himself) and delighted most of us. It is an assignment to set the seal on a great career, and in his accomplishment of it he certainly did not let anyone down. Henry Blofeld took the BBC mantle from him in time for the first tour defeat, in the first first-class match. Ian Botham had not been too much in the limelight thus far, but the announcement of his signing for Queensland for the next two years came on the day that state beat*

England. For once the team must have been grateful for the media obsession with their big all-rounder which drew attention away from the unfortunate result. Victory over South Australia followed, although the detractors were quick to point out that here was the least penetrative Sheffield Shield attack. Then it was westward to Perth and a particularly unconvincing display against Western Australia which, though they managed a draw, earned England the tag of a side that couldn't bat, couldn't bowl, and couldn't field. We were to remember that over the weeks that followed.

That Western Australia match was the first fixture of the tour for Christopher Martin-Jenkins. He had been given his final briefings and been equipped, like James Bond by 'Q', with gadgets for improving telephone quality, microphones, tape recorder and of course plenty of paperwork. England were heading for the First Test in Brisbane as he made the first entry in this tour log, not subsequently amended.

Thursday 13 November, Brisbane It is difficult to envisage England winning the First Test which starts in Brisbane tomorrow, but you never know. I feel rather less pessimistic than most of my colleagues, perhaps because I have been here only a week and have seen only one bad performance, not two. Many touring sides have done worse than this going into the First Test, but the silly thing is that England have had only three first-class games in five weeks in the country. Those who framed the itinerary have got their priorities wrong, yet again.

Experience may pull England through, however, especially if they have some luck with the toss. Australia are very short of Test experience, especially in bowling, although their batting now seems to have a much more solid look. If the pitch here plays as it usually does, and it looks green enough, the toss may be crucial. The winning captain is certain to put the other side in, unless it is a burning hot day which in today's humid and cloudy weather looks unlikely.

Contrary to many recent reports, England are not in a state of disintegration and they have a much more realistic hope of doing well in this match than they had approaching the opening match of their last overseas rubber in Jamaica last February. But they need sharper fielding, especially in the slips, and much more disciplined batting than they showed during embarrassing collapses against Queensland (who beat them) and Western Australia (who probably would have won too but for the weather). The failure of Slack, Gower, Gatting and Athey to make even a fifty is extremely worrying. Since Athey has had only two failures to Slack's four, the former will no doubt go in first with Broad and there is a possibility that Gatting will bat at number three instead of Gower, to protect that often rather fragile genius from the fury of Australia's new-ball bowlers.

The uncertainty over the batting means that the Surrey wicketkeeper Jack Richards, along with the talented and rapidly developing DeFreitas, is likely to win his first cap tomorrow at the expense of French, who has good reason to feel poorly treated after some immaculate performances behind the stumps last summer. Richards is certainly a better batsman and, if a lesser wicketkeeper, he is unlikely to let anyone down.

Australia's chances have improved as a result of their recent short but tough tour in India. Although they did not win, they managed not to be beaten, thus stopping a rot which was every bit as deep as the one affecting England. Border now seems a relaxed and confident captain and the emergence of Dean Jones, who scored a momentous double hundred in Madras, as the team's number three has taken the pressure off Border. Above these two, Boon and Marsh have begun to establish themselves as an opening pair, and below them, Ritchie, Matthews and Waugh are all good cricketers.

Australia's bowling is less strong. Lawson is returning after a long absence as a result of injury, Hughes is fast but straightforward, Greg Matthews an unexceptional off-spinner and his namesake Chris, although strong and promising, is very inexperienced. The danger-man is Reid, surely the thinnest man ever to bowl fast for Australia, but at six foot eight inches with an action which makes the most of his height, a difficult proposition, especially for batsmen who have been non-plussed by the unusual angle of the left-arm-over bowlers.

C.M-J.

Thursday 13 November, London Working on the home end of *Test Match Special* from Australia is a question of the jet lag without the suntan. Indeed it was a wet autumn evening as I left home after a meal which I called breakfast and my wife called supper. I had managed two or three hours' sleep in the afternoon and now the excitement of an imminent Ashes series was taking over.

Play was due to start at 12.30 p.m. GMT and finish at 7.30 in the morning, so we have decided to take commentary on the first and last sessions, as a lunch interval at half past two in the morning is certain to lose us most of our audience. There will also be hourly reports for Radio 2 through the night and several for Radio 4 during the latter stages of each day's play as Britain awakes, anxious for the news from Down Under. *Test Match Special* will be taking the Australian Broadcasting Corporation's commentary, a reversion to the more traditional policy after having staged our own broadcast on the last England tour there. Joining a broadcast over which you have no control presents its own problems and we had some interesting moments. Just before midnight Christopher rang from a bright, sunny morning in Brisbane and we went through the final arrangements. Twenty-five minutes into Friday morning a Radio 3 announcer anxious to be away to his bed handed over to me and in studio B8, two floors underground in Broadcasting House, the TMS signature tune, 'Florida Fantasy' started to play as in Brisbane England's new opening pair, Broad and Athey, pulled on their gloves and donned their helmets as they left the cool shade of the dressing-room for the centre of the Gabba ground and what all Australians and quite a few Englishmen expected to be a roasting at the hands of the Australian bowlers.

At 2.00 a.m. the first wrinkle in our system showed when we were suddenly and unexpectedly treated to an ABC news bulletin. Not knowing what to expect, I quickly leaped to the microphone to fill in with a summary of the previous hour and a half's play until I could hear in my headphones the newsreader return listeners to the ground.

Through the still watches of the night the news seemed better for English ears than we have dared to hope, as Athey and Gatting put on a century second wicket partnership. So it was a pleasure to be able to awaken people at 5.25 a.m. with news of a satisfactory first four hours of the series. I could have wished for a smoother start to our second *TMS* session. I had been told to expect a countdown from Brisbane to the start of the post-tea commentary, which I would hear in my headphones as a direct feed from the commentary box. As the signature tune faded away and I started to speak, I could hear Christopher giving the promised countdown: 'We shall start in one minute from now'.

I checked the clock and started my stopwatch while reading the day's details so far. Half a minute later, as you might expect, I heard, 'Starting in 30 seconds'. 'No!' another voice chipped in at the other end, throwing everything into total confusion.

As an argument raged in my headphones I floundered on awaiting its outcome: 'The commentary team is Jim Maxwell, Neville Oliver, Norman O'Neill . . .'

At last I heard a positive 'Starting in ten seconds'. '. . . and the first voice we shall hear is Christopher Martin-Jenkins', I concluded with relief, closing my microphone. To my astonishment I heard a fanfare and a recorded voice introducing 'ABC cricket from the Gabba'. I will know next time!

P.B.

There was one further hiccup on that first day when rain stopped play in the last 40 minutes and the ABC decided to go into a phone-in. The commentators even suggested that some callers might like to ring from Britain. Thus encouraged, I decided to stay with it but as they asked the first caller to put his question it became apparent that we would not be hearing that end of the conversation. So we never found out if there were any British contributors as we resorted to the more traditional TMS *solution to rain breaks – music. There was a little more play before the close by which time England must have been very pleased with a score of 198 for 2.*

The start of the second day gave those who waited up at home some anxious moments as both Lamb and Athey went without adding to their scores. Radio 1's Andy Peebles, joining me in the studio for some midnight company, was biting his nails as hard as anyone as David Gower was dropped without scoring. But the ship was righted and when I re-started the network after the tea interval it was with the news that Gower had made 50 and Ian Botham, after an afternoon session of pure destruction, was 119 not out. There was a little more of his innings for early morning listeners to enjoy and also the fine contribution of a newcomer – Phillip DeFreitas.

England's dismissal for 456 – after being put in – left Australia over an hour of the second day to bat and DeFreitas time to follow his 40 runs with his first Test wicket.

In the early hours of Sunday morning it was music to Pommie ears to hear the last five wickets go quickly and Australia commence their second innings following on. Someone had misread the Australian marketing men's script.

Five Australian second innings wickets were down on the fourth day so we decided that we would take the whole of the final day's commentary. BBC Television, too, decided to take the first session of play, which, while it gave us competition, provided me with some very welcome pictures to keep me company during the lonely vigil. In the event they were also to prove a life-saver shortly after England had made the breakthrough with the vital wicket of Geoff Marsh for 110. There followed one of the irritating breaks in the satellite circuit which had occurred throughout the Test. This one, though, sounded more prolonged so I glanced at my television set to start commentary from the studio. As I looked at it I saw a wicket fall.

'Emburey's bowled him!' I declared, and then had an awful thought: was it an action replay? As I recalled that Emburey had not yet bowled anyone in that innings it had to be live, I also had to identify which of the two identically helmeted and unfamiliar Australian batsmen – each conveniently with his back to the camera – was out. As I plumped for Zoehrer, the shot of Waugh walking back to the pavilion came up. Happily so did the line from Brisbane, so after trying to sort out the confusion I returned to the commentary and reached for a strong black coffee.

Australia's collapse gained momentum and at 3.46 a.m. Christopher was able to describe England's first Test win of 1986 and that gave him something to reflect on in his journal as he headed next day for Newcastle.

Thursday 20 November, en route to Newcastle A neat cartoon on the front page of the Murdoch national paper, *The Australian*, summed up the generally rather cynical press reaction to Australia's seven-wicket defeat by England in the First Test at Brisbane. It depicts Allan Border barking at a laconic-looking journalist: 'I'm sick of you knockers in the media – haven't I won eight tosses in a row?'

The press are calling Border 'grumpy' and unfortunately this is exactly what he was yesterday in reacting not so much to his team's poor performance and England's excellent one as to the criticism of his captaincy. Border will gain nothing by being ratty with the media. It is unfair to blame the captain for Australia's poor start when it is his batting that has so often saved them from total collapse in the last two years. He is not, it is true, a very imaginative captain, but if his bowlers don't bowl consistently straight to a good length, as England's, with Emburey and Dilley to the fore, certainly did, it is not the captain's fault. Border's problem is probably simply that he is tired and that tired people get angry. He should not have been asked to lead an eight-week tour to India immediately before a long, arduous season at home. And he probably should not have played a season for Essex.

England travelled to Newcastle today for their four-day match against New South Wales, happy to let Australia worry about their problems and determined to build on their good start to the Test series. Any danger of complacency ought to be banished by a reminder that no opening partnership in eight first-class innings on tour has exceeded 15. The four players who missed the match at the Gabba; Foster, French, Slack and Small, are in the 12 and the New South Wales team will include two bowlers, Geoff Lawson and Mike Whitney, anxious to catch the eyes of the Australian selectors.

C.M-J.

In a windswept Newcastle Whitney, at least, made his point with seven wickets in an embarrassingly abrupt England defeat by eight wickets.

Wednesday 26 November, Perth If there was no panic among the Australian selectors in reaction to England's first Test victory, there has been none either in the England camp as a result of the defeat in two and a half days by New South Wales. There was talk at first of voluntary net practice only today but I understand this has now become a little more formal: eight players will have a net today under Micky Stewart and the other eight tomorrow afternoon, while everyone will have a full-scale session on Wednesday and Thursday mornings. It was the young, keen ones – including the captain – who were at the nets today. No Botham, Gower or Lamb!

No doubt there will be those who think that after such a woeful performance in Newcastle the whip should have been cracked a little harder and everyone made to get out and sweat under the hot Perth sun, but I have not been given the impression, at this stage of the tour anyway, that the priorities are wrong, and under Stewart's careful guidance those who might prefer an easier life are being made to work hard enough without becoming stale. Fitness is also the concern, of course, of the team's respected physiotherapist, Laurie Brown, the quiet man from Mussel-burgh known as 'Haggis', who has helped to keep the team, so far, free of any serious injury.

I went along to look at the WACA this morning and was impressed by the perfect condition of the outfield. At this stage, too, the pitch under John Maley's dedicated supervision looks very well prepared and less green than Brisbane. It has been unpredictable, I am told, since it was relaid two years ago, but I would be surprised if bowlers don't have to work hard this time: one reason, perhaps, why Australia are likely to follow England's example and go into the match with two spinners. They have won three Tests in their last 29 and on each occasion the leg-spin of Bob Holland has been largely responsible. He is a bigger spinner of the ball, though, than Peter Sleep, so England will be hoping, like Macbeth, to murder Sleep!

C.M–J.

Friday 28 November, London I always feel that Perth has the best hours of play for our broadcasting of any of the overseas grounds. The day starts at an inhospitable 3.00 a.m., but it ends at 10.00 a.m. having given people a taste of sunshine at their breakfast table and packed them off to work. Our plan here was to carry commentary on the last two sessions, starting at 5.35 a.m., and again we were able to wake our English audience with good news. England had rattled off to a fine start thanks to an opening partnership between Broad and Athey which eventually made 223.

With tea intervals to fill throughout this Test and Christmas fast approaching, I ran a daily feature on the recent cricket publications which included interviews with one or two of the authors. I was particularly pleasantly surprised by the reaction to one of the interviews – with E.W. Swanton, who had just produced a third edition of *Barclay's World of Cricket*. His thoughts on the state of the game – as sound as ever – gave a rise to a number of letters applauding his attitude to many of the current trends and particularly to those which seemed to be changing the emphasis of the game in Australia.

Circuit problems with Perth are not unknown, as there is an awful lot of Australia between Perth and the satellite station in Sydney. These days that part of the chain is also by satellite which is considerably more reliable than the old land lines. The only serious break came on the the third day, a ten-minute interruption during which I read every piece of paper in front of me, barely stopping short of the maker's name on the studio clock. It was very good, therefore, on the final day, when England had set Australia 390 to win, to have live television pictures again. The sunshine sparkling on the Swan River beyond the WACA ground in such vivid colours looked so alluring it was hard to believe the vision was coming all the way from the other side of the world.

P.B.

Wednesday 3 December, Perth The groundsman won. It was touch and go whether Australia would avoid the follow-on and even on the last day there were moments when England had chances of forcing a victory. But although the pitch took on the appearance, in close-up, of a huge jig-saw puzzle – sporting the biggest cracks I have seen since Sabina Park in 1973–74, another drawn game – it remained rock-hard and by care and determination Australia, aided by faulty England tactics, managed to draw and so to keep the series very much alive.

England, however, had dominated the match for threequarters of its course after a serene and impressive maiden Test hundred by Broad, a dogged innings by Athey and a majestic one by Gower. How good it was to see him playing so brilliantly again.

Gatting had decided against declaring half an hour before the end of the fourth day, feeling that England had not scored quite quickly enough to justify giving Australia even the slightest sniff of a target within range. But he did declare the following morning, thus wasting the chance of finding out whether a further squashing with the heavy roller might have caused the huge cracks in the pitch to start crumbling.

Gatting was too slow to get Emburey and Edmonds on in harness and opened after lunch with Dilley and Botham, instead of keeping the spinners on and giving himself a greater chance with the second new ball with fresher fast bowlers. Two balls through his seventh over, Botham broke down with a side injury and for a wasted period Gatting used DeFreitas and himself to containing fields as if he was seriously worried about Australia's getting the runs. This had to be wrong. Indeed if Australia had become interested in victory it would only have increased England's chances of bowling them out. But Ritchie and Matthews kept their heads down and their bats straight and Australia completed their very important escape. Test cricket in Australia would have suffered a long-term blow had England gone two up with three to play. A draw guaranteed bigger gates at Adelaide than the poor ones at Brisbane and the modest ones at Perth.

C.M-J.

Saturday 6 December, Melbourne England discovered to their horror on arriving at the ground for their match against Victoria that their captain was not among them. He arrived after David Gower had lost the toss and taken over the captaincy in the field. After an early statement that Gatting had been indisposed, the management wisely decided to reveal the truth which was simply that he had overslept. Gatting was obviously very embarrassed and, although not too much should be made of this, it might be a timely lesson to him not to let standards slip at a crucial period of the tour: next week's potentially decisive Test at Adelaide looms. Since the injured Botham will not be able to bowl, Gatting's 4 for 31 in 14 bustling overs as Victoria were dismissed for 101 was significant, although Foster, with 3 for 29, and Small, with 3 for 30, were the real destroyers on a bad wicket.

C.M-J.

England went on to win that match by five wickets and headed for Adelaide and the Third Test.

Thursday 11 December, Adelaide The tension so evident in the England camp before the First Test in Brisbane has returned as the team prepares for what must be a crucial third match in Adelaide tomorrow. If Australia do not win here, they will need to take both the last two Tests to regain the Ashes, but because of the injury to Ian Botham and the small cloud which blew up over Mike Gatting's head at the start of the win against Victoria, there seems to be almost as much pressure on England not to lose as there is on Australia to win.

The affair of Rip Van Gatting is perhaps best viewed from an Australian point. As the team took off on their flight from Melbourne to Adelaide, the stewardess reading out the safety instructions concluded thus: 'Finally, ladies and gentlemen, I have a request from the England captain, Mr Gatting. During this flight he asks that you should all talk quietly so that he may get some sleep'. Laughter all round was the response and the balanced judgment of one of Australia's senior cricket writers, Alan Shiell, was: 'If it weren't so funny and inconsequential, it would be serious'.

I would back Gatting to silence his insomniac critics by making a major personal contribution, perhaps in the form of his seventh Test hundred, at the Adelaide Oval, a lovely ground to make runs on. The pitch, on first inspection, looks likely to be true, barring interruptions from the weather, which is so unpredictable at the moment that last weekend a near cyclone ripped part of the roofing off one of the stands. It now seems virtually certain that England will be without Botham. The torn muscle in his side still hurts when he coughs or sneezes, so the business of swinging his heavy cricket bat, let alone swinging his own heavy frame into delivering a ball, is too painful seriously to contemplate.

Although it is asking a lot of Gatting to operate as the third seamer and the stock bowler, especially as Dilley and DeFreitas are by no means an established new-ball pair, the odds are that Edmonds and Emburey will be doing much of the bowling anyway. It seems, therefore, that the hour may have come for 24-year-old James Whitaker. He has flair and his innings against Victoria at Melbourne on Tuesday was marked by several strokes of brilliant timing. On that Melbourne pitch of uneven bounce his hooking was rash, but it helps his chances of selection that he made a most confident 108 at the Adelaide Oval last month.

C.M-J.

Friday 12 December, London For the Adelaide Test we reverted to the same UK hours of play as for the First Test in Brisbane. The time difference with Adelaide – ten and a hour hours ahead of GMT – is always a hard one to work out quickly if, like me, you are bad at mental arithmetic.

I gave up my seat at the microphone in the *Test Match Special* studio for this match to Ron Jones, more usually a soccer commentator, but a passionate cricket devotee and frequent commentator on the game during his time with Radio Wales. He was also at one stage involved with coaching young West Indians in Jamaica when he was a schoolmaster there. His presence left me with the leg-work of producing the output from the Test match on three networks, dashing between *Test Match Special* in the Broadcasting House basement, Radio 2 for the hourly reports on the first floor and Radio 4 News on the third floor. With play starting on the odd half-hour, I was able to set Ron off with *TMS* before going to Radio 2 to raise Christopher on the telephone for his 1.00 a.m. report. I envied him his position there at my favourite Australian Test ground.

This first day he watched Australia's batsmen on top after winning the toss. Boon, his place having looked shaky in the side, made 103 and only two wickets fell.

P.B.

Australia declared late on the second day at 514 for 5 but England, too, started with yet another century opening partnership, Broad making his second hundred in successive Tests and Gatting following it with another. After three days England were 165 behind with five wickets in hand.

Sunday 14 December, Adelaide I write this on the bank of the River Torrens with the Adelaide Oval not much more than a six-hit away across the river and the bells of the Cathedral still calling the faithful to evensong, less than two weeks before Christmas. Peter Baxter has just said goodbye down the line from London, prior to a drive home over icy roads in the cold December dawn. Here it is a bright, lovely evening, a cool breeze blowing on the back of my neck but the sun still warm on a face which, cooped up in a commentary box by day and a hotel by night, has seen little fresh air since the day before the match when I managed to play an enjoyable foursome at Royal Adelaide with Tony Lewis, Patrick Eagar and the Secretary of the Adelaide Club, Brian Gardiner.

The Third Test match is heading for a draw, 863 runs so far and only five wickets for each side. England are still 165 behind and batted rather carelessly in the final session today, but they ought to be safe from defeat. Young James Whitaker has a chance for glory tomorrow on as good a wicket as he will ever play on in what may be a long Test career.

Gatting played the innings of the day today, in fact the innings of the match, 100 off 140 balls with 15 fours. He made Matthews look the friendly off-spinner he is, and dealt more confidently than any of the others with Sleep, the leg-spinner, whose presence added interest to an otherwise fairly predictable day. Broad made another hundred too, but I was especially pleased for Gatting, who had been sorely embarrassed – and rightly so – by his failure to appear at the start of last Saturday's match against Victoria. Oversleeping after a late night is not a good example for a captain to set but it will only seriously be used in evidence against him if England do not win the Ashes. His hundred today won me £20 for a friendly wager with John Thicknesse. (I sometimes seem to have a premonition about these things and nearly asked Thickers for his quote on a Broad hundred before Perth!)

It is a shame there is no Rest Day tomorrow. I had a migraine soon after our arrival from Adelaide which was due, no doubt, to a build-up of weariness. Everyone involved in a Test, especially the players, needs a rest after three days, and we shall all miss the traditional visit to the Yalumba Winery in the Barrossa Valley. The last two days of this match will be long and wearisome.

C.M-J.

As predicted, that match was drawn. England batted past the middle of the fourth day for 455, which left time only really for Border to record yet another Test hundred before the game was dead.

The next day Christopher was off with the England team to the Apple Isle . . .

Mike Gatting sheds his Rip Van Winkle image with a century at Adelaide.
All-Sport/Adrian Murrell

Wednesday 17 December, Hobart It is a real joy to have arrived in Tasmania after the hectic and unrelenting pace of this tour so far. Here one really might be in Scotland or, since we are on the Derwent, the Lake District and, just to complete the sudden feeling of being in a home from home, it was pouring with rain as we all arrived after a delayed flight from Adelaide, and a pretty bouncy one at that, as Australia's unusually unsummery summer continues.

Tasmania, especially Hobart here in the South, has never been renowned for hot weather, of course, and when the Indians came here for their match this time last year not a ball was bowled over the four days.

It has rained enough, I gather, in recent days for a delayed start and interruptions from the weather to be probable rather than possible, which would be a pity – and not just because in fine weather the TCA ground at Hobart ranks amongst the most beautiful in the world, with mountain on one side and river on the other.

Tasmania hold their own in the Sheffield Shield these days and have a menacing opening attack spearheaded by a young tearaway fast bowler picturesquely named Troy Cooley – allow me to be the first to call him the Trojan Horse – and a certain Richard Ellison. The word is that the Kent all-rounder, who would have been in my 16 for Australia regardless of last season's form, has got his swing back.

It is an important game for him if he wants to prove the point, as I'm sure he does, and an important one too for all those on the fringe of England's Test side. This is the last first-class match on the tour apart from the Fourth and Fifth Tests.

In the end Ellison bowled well, but England won easily, with John Emburey hitting 46 entirely in boundaries – ten fours and a six: a record.

C.M-J.

Tuesday 23 December, Hobart The widely anticipated return of Craig McDermott, who took 30 wickets in six Tests in England in 1985, will make it less likely that England can continue the extraordinary succession of batting indulgences against Australia when the Third Test starts in Melbourne on Boxing Day. One can really hardly believe the truth when one thinks how embarrassingly frail England's batting has so often been in recent seasons against all other Test opposition. But facts, M'lud, are indisputedly facts. In this series alone, England's first innings scores have been: 456, 392 for 8, and 455. In England last time, McDermott notwithstanding, they were 533 (the absent Robinson made 175), 290 (in the lost Lord's Test), 456, 257 (in the Old Trafford draw), 595 and 464.

It is difficult to think of any period in history when England's batsmen have so enjoyed themselves at Australia's expense. It was not always so, but to score heavily in the first innings of a Test match is, these days, at the very least an insurance against defeat. Therefore, if England can manage it once more at the MCG, the largest and in some ways the most daunting cricket stadium in the world (though Calcutta now comes close in both respects), they will assure themselves of the still hallowed Ashes.

After two matches in which the captain winning the toss has not hesitated a second before deciding to bat, the crucial 22 yards of the MCG's still slightly motley square will be very closely inspected this time. If there is some moisture on or just under the surface, Australia will at last have an attack capable of using it well.

The current Australian script is that an improving national team will spend the weekend after Christmas belatedly putting the Poms in their place before going on to steal the Ashes by winning the final Test in Sydney on a spinner's pitch. But England have no reason to listen to the propaganda. Although it would be bad for the finances of Australian cricket, and indeed for Test cricket generally here, which is in danger of being run over and squashed into oblivion by the one-day juggernaut, they have only to get one more good start to spoil the scenario.

Botham will return at number six and England's third seamer, and the only new contender for a place in the final XI is Foster, who has been having a good tour and has steadily pressed DeFreitas for his place.

C.M-J.

Boxing Day, Friday 26 December, London With a Test match starting on Boxing Day, touring cricketers generally have a 'no drink after four o'clock' rule on Christmas Day. The presenter of *Test Match Special* is subject to a similar, though less severe restriction, 12,000 miles away. Eleven o'clock on Boxing Day morning in Melbourne is midnight on Christmas night in Britain and so for me it was a case of watching the Queen's Christmas message on television and trying to grab a few hours' sleep before driving into London on unnaturally deserted roads. The pavements of the capital were similarly empty, left only to the most committed: two joggers and a handful of dog-walkers.

Broadcasting House makes only a few concessions to the festive season. A tree in the foyer, an offensive-tie contest in the Newsroom where they are determined to find a use for some of their Christmas presents, and a paper hat or two in the Control Room. Otherwise it is business as usual.

Having sent our audience to bed at 2.00 a.m. with three Australian wickets down at lunch, it was remarkable to be able to wake them early for the start of England's first innings. Seven wickets had fallen between lunch and tea and the heroes were Gladstone Small in his first Test of the series and, almost inevitably, Ian Botham; back to near-fitness, but bowling off a restricted run-up.

P.B.

Sunday 28 December, London England had gained a first innings lead of 208 at the end of the second day, so, remembering the Australian Boxing Day collapse, I arranged to continue the commentary throughout the night if three of their second innings wickets were down by lunch.

Fifty minutes before the interval there were two down, so until the last ball of the session was bowled we could not be sure of our plans. It remained two wickets and at the interval I spent some time working out the list of reports required for the next day. It was not to be needed.

The end came so swiftly that one could barely keep up with noting the details of each wicket. The last five wickets fell in just 39 minutes after tea and by 5.40 on that Sunday morning – probably before most of our audience had surfaced – England had made sure of winning the series and the Ashes had been retained. The suddenness of it caught most people on the hop, but it was a happy way to end the Christmas holiday, not least for me, with the knowledge that I could have an extra couple of nights in bed.

P.B.

Christopher summed up his thoughts on the victory in this despatch . . .

Monday 29 December, Melbourne England's first Test victory inside three days at Melbourne since 1901 yesterday has made certain of both the Ashes and the series. Australians are today forgetting the Test match and thinking instead either about the Davis Cup, which they won triumphantly a few hours before surrendering the Ashes, or the America's Cup, which they still hold.

But they cannot hide from the facts of their innings and 14-run defeat at the MCG. Bob Hawke, the Prime Minister, said at a Davis Cup dinner last night that 'if there is anything worse than a whingeing Pom it is a gloating Pom'. This particular Pom found their defeat almost embarrassing. True followers of the game here are wondering whether Sri Lanka, who lack experience overseas but certainly not talent, or Australia currently hold the wooden spoon of international cricket.

Two things have contributed to their current malaise, and neither is without a parallel in the United Kingdom. The first is the impoverishment of Australia's reserve strength through the enticement of several of the nation's best players by South Africa. Cricketers like Kim Hughes and Terry Alderman are not replaced overnight and even if there are not many players currently engaged in South Africa who would necessarily be involved in the Ashes series, their absence nevertheless reduces the pool of available players and weakens the competition in the Sheffield Shield, the training-ground for Test cricketers.

The second factor goes back further than the South African intrusions. Australia indulges in far too much cricket of a flippant, insignificant and forgettable nature. I refer of course to the absurd excess of limited-overs internationals which every season here since World Series Cricket reached an uneasy truce with the Australian Cricket Board in 1979 has received star billing from those who promote the game, ostensibly in the interests of 'cricket' but primarily in the interests of no one but themselves.

If pride will have its fall, greed will have equally painful consequences. I have suggested before that world administrators should abandon their obsession with money-making and agree to a self-denying ordinance by which each country would agree to a maximum number of Tests and One-Day Internationals in any year. Australia, by far the worst culprits, need to diet themselves more than anyone.

Indeed, it is precisely the fact that so many Tests are played that Australia's team now appears to be worse than it actually is. It is only a few months since England were being beaten at home by India and New Zealand and a few months further back to the horrors of the Caribbean. If they were to leave for the West Indies tomorrow, the England team in their current mood and form, with Mike Gatting as captain and the increasingly influential Micky Stewart cracking the whip when necessary as cricket manager, England might draw a game or two against by far the best side in the world. They would almost certainly have little trouble in reversing last season's results against the other two countries.

There is much tiring cricket to come on this tour, including the Fifth Test in Sydney, for which England will start warm favourites. For the moment, though, we should salute those who have brought home the Ashes. Gatting's captaincy has lived up to my own expectations of it and confounded many pundits who failed to see his qualities. He is no genius, but a tough little nut and a real cricketer. Botham has never had a more effective overseas tour. Gower is enjoying his cricket again and playing it well. Edmonds and Emburey have done what was expected of them, not least in the second innings at Melbourne when they hustled through Australia's middle and late order with confidence and authority. Broad's third hundred in successive Tests has put him among very exalted company indeed. Athey has grafted nobly as his partner. Small had a marvellous match as a replacement for the injured Dilley, and Richards was as brilliant behind the stumps here as he was with the bat at Perth.

Maybe it is true that a mediocre team has beaten a poor one. But the Ashes are the Ashes and after a year in which England spent much of the time licking its own wounds, Mr Hawke will have to excuse the gloating Poms who have come to his country to celebrate the New Year. What a pity that reality is likely to reassert itself when England face West Indies in one of those interminable One-Day Internationals later this week!

C.M-J.

Thursday 1 January, London England and Australia have now taken wing again across the vastness of the continent to Perth for the quadrangular tournament of One-Day Internationals which form part of the America's Cup festivities. It has been very difficult to assess in advance what sort of interest will be engendered at home by these matches. We decided to carry hourly reports on Radio 2 and to do commentary on the final if England should reach it. Back in August, when we laid the plans, that seemed scarcely a probability, but that was before the Ashes were so firmly secured. Pakistan, too, started the tournament with a shock win over the West Indies. Today the Poms continued their Aussie-bashing with a 37-run victory.

P.B.

Saturday 3 January, London Cricket seems to be the centre of attention over what is for many people still the Christmas holiday, and BBC Television caught the mood with a decision to broadcast the second half of today's England versus West Indies match live. Not, of course, that we had any doubt that in this game the bubble would burst. Indeed, when Christopher spoke to me before his first report he said, 'This is a different game'. England were 10 for 2 in the fourth over; Marshall and Garner were in business again. Lamb fought back, though, with 71 and the score was respectable, if not, one felt, quite enough at 228 for 9 in 50 overs.

The television planners were to be well rewarded for their decision to follow the West Indies' attempt on that target. Despite a lack of radio commentary, Radio 4's new Saturday *Today* programme, launched today, kept abreast of developments, as did Cliff Morgan in his *Sport on Four* programme. I discovered a knot of West Indian-born members of the canteen staff grouped anxiously round a television set as the crucial moment of Viv Richards' demise – caught on the boundary off Emburey – seemed to turn the tide in England's favour.

It seemed later that when the final West Indian wicket fell to give England victory by 19 runs the entire nation had been watching. The euphoria, good though the win undoubtedly is, and significant in laying a bogey, seems rather out of proportion, but that is the power of live television. This victory, too, was ideally timed, ending at 10.30 a.m. this morning. It makes one wonder whether we missed a trick by not carrying radio commentary on it. It is possible to argue that with the benefit of hindsight, but it would have been justified only as an adjunct to a television spectacular. I tried to convey to Christopher the impact that the success for England has had – even in as forgettable a tournament as this 'Perth Challenge'. At least we have been given early notice that we will now be mounting a commentary on Wednesday for the final.

P.B.

Wednesday 7 January, London Something of the climax of the tournament has been dissipated by the fact that England and Pakistan met two days ago in what had become by then an academic exercise. They also had the bad taste, one felt, to mis-read the marketing men's script. It should have been Australia versus the West Indies for the final or, just as a barely acceptable possibility, Australia versus England. The final that did take place was only just kept a contest by the batting of Javed Miandad with 77 not out, and by England's rapid loss of two wickets in their pursuit of 167 to win. But they got there for the loss of five wickets with nearly ten overs to spare.

P.B.

Thursday 8 January, en route to Sydney For someone delighted to see England winning cricket matches again out of habit, yet convinced that too many tournaments like this one will only devalue still further the currency of international cricket, it was impossible not to be ambivalent about England's sweeping victory in the Perth Challenge.

It was an outstandingly successful promotion, if judged in isolation from the remainder of the Australian season. The WACA is a splendid setting for cricket in its modernised form; the weather was hot and sunny throughout; the organisation was slick and professional; the pitches were generally excellent; and five of the seven matches produced exciting finishes, a very high proportion. Crowds were large and profits high, despite generous prize-money, the lion's share of which was collected by Mike Gatting and his businesslike team. But this was, nonetheless, a superfluous competition organised as part of a general Festival of Sport to coincide with the America's Cup, which is much more about big business and showbusiness than it is about sport. Fortunes are being made, and a few more lost on the America's Cup. The very economy of Western Australia was heavily dependent on whether or not the challenging yacht was American. There will be far more big-spending Americans than there will be New Zealanders.

The Perth Challenge competition was agreed to by overseas administrators, anxious neither to offend the PBL and the ACB nor to miss any of the large profits still available in a land where patience has not yet, apparently, been lost by the public with limited-overs cricket, even when Australia are being beaten.

Those same administrators, from England, the West Indies and Pakistan, were in Perth to enjoy the sunshine and to be 'wined and dined' by the home authority. Next stop Sharjah in April for another four-nation competition. More profits; more easy money for the players. But who in future will really care, or even remember, except those who were there, who won the Perth Challenge? And will it not render much less significant the World Cup, assuming it eventually takes place, in India and Pakistan later this year?

England were quite clearly the outstanding team of the tournament. To win a final with as many as nine overs and five balls to spare with five wickets in hand was a very substantial achievement. But the true test of England's improvement during this tour will be measured by their ability to repeat their superiority over the West Indies during the long round of World Series Internationals which follow the Fifth Test.

That final Test starts in Sydney on Saturday. England have now won six matches in a row since defeating Tasmania just before Christmas and only carelessness can prevent them from extending the sequence here and writing a 3–0 victory into the record books. They were always expected to win at Melbourne and Sydney, even before the tour began. What had not been envisaged was the opening success at Brisbane which had such a wonderful effect on England's morale and was so wounding for Allan Border and his disappointing team.

C.M-J.

Thursday 15 January, London Before we went on the air at midnight for the last day of the Test series the decision was already taken that we would take commentary through the night for the whole day's play. England needed 281 runs in the day to win the match with nine wickets still standing. In fact I had made a late decision to continue after lunch when England's bowlers had had a good morning and

Australia, with seven wickets down, were 213 runs ahead. It had been a remarkable match for the final one of a dead series. Jones' single-handed effort in Australia's first innings had been capped by the fairytale performance of the unknown Peter Taylor – 53 runs and six wickets so far. We had had some Gower elegance (disgracefully ignored by the Channel 9 Television highlights) and some Emburey unorthodoxy. Now all results were possible.

The day ebbed and flowed and the tension mounted – no less in Studio B8 than at the SCG. Just after 6.00 a.m. GMT the last 20 overs were begun with England needing 90 runs from their last five wickets and appropriately their pugnacious captain was still there and dominating proceedings. If he stayed anything was possible, but in the second over of those last 20 he fell for 96. The tension did not end with that, but now it was just a question of whether or not England could hold on. They only just failed to – Emburey was finally beaten by one that kept low from Sleep in the penultimate over. Australia had won by 55 runs and regained their self-respect.

P.B.

Friday 16 January, Sydney Cricket's essential unpredictability was never more classically illustrated than it was in both the final Test at Sydney and in the Ashes series as a whole. At Sydney an England team buoyant from victories in their previous six games was confident that, if the pitch turned as much as it had in all recent Test matches at the SCG, they had in Emburey and Edmonds spinners superior to Sleep, who had made little impact as a leg-spinner in his previous six Tests, and Taylor, who had made very little impact with *anyone* bar a few percipient people in more than a decade of faithful weekend cricket for the Grade team Northern District. If anyone was going to be plucked from obscurity, followers of Sydney Grade cricket would have expected it to be a left-arm spinner called Whitfield, who has always been more highly rated than Taylor. But Greg Chappell, the most influential of the Australian selection committee, had seen enough of Taylor in last season's Sheffield Shield final to want to have him in the Queensland team. Taylor, with a family business to look after, stayed in his native city.

When the script for the Ashes series was written on the eve of the First Test in November, it suggested that Australia, with two left-arm-over bowlers to exploit England's apparent weakness against that form of attack, and a settled batting order worked out on a successful tour of India, would be too good for the England team lacking confidence after a wretched 1986. But by the end of the tour the experience of Edmonds and Emburey would be starting to tell, the pundits said, and with these two in the side England were favourites to win in Sydney.

As we all now know, exactly the reverse happened. England excelled themselves at Brisbane, helped by a vital contribution from their admirably assertive captain on

Wicketkeeper Jack Richards justified the *in only his second Test.*
tour selectors' faith with a century at Perth All-Sport/Adrian Murrell

the first morning of the series, and they had no serious early batting collapse until the final match. Get a settled pair of opening batsmen and you are halfway to winning any cricket match. Broad and Athey did an excellent job throughout against bowling which was seldom very testing by the highest standards, the gangling Reid (with 20 wickets at 26 the highest wicket-taker in the series) excepted. Gower, who had started the tour both unhappy and out of form, recovered his beautiful touch after being dropped before he had scored at the Gabba. Gower, Gatting and, fitfully but memorably – especially at Brisbane – Botham, made the most of the good starts. Only Lamb was out of luck and when Gooch returns next summer there will probably be no place for him.

Australia's batting was at least the equal of England's and in Marsh, Jones, Border, Ritchie and Waugh there are strong bricks for future building. Where England proved far superior – or at least superior enough – was in the field. Richards was clearly the better of two wicket-keepers, neither of whom are quite out of the highest drawer, and his batting was splendidly confident and assertive. Sad though one feels for the unfortunate French, Richards was an inspired selection, one missed stumping at Sydney – a vital one it is true – being his only serious mistake.

The bowlers did just enough and gave the Australians fewer easy runs. Dilley, sadly, was still unable to get through a whole series without injury but he at last took five wickets in an innings and bowled consistently dangerously with the new ball. Small bowled best of all the fast bowlers and proved in the last two Tests that he should have been playing all along, for all DeFreitas's still maturing abilities. Edmonds and Emburey lived up to their reputations as good, accurate spin bowlers, Edmonds proving again that he can be a good and useful team man, despite what Willis and Brearley used to think. Emburey recovered well from a mid-tour loss of confidence and rhythm to take his first seven-wicket haul at Sydney.

And then there was Botham. On his last tour he has committed himself whole-heartedly to the cause, behaved like a contented family man and, although his figures have in the end been no great improvement on those of many other overseas tours, he has been continuously useful. Full marks, too, to the tour leaders. Micky Stewart has played a blinder, using just the right amount of carrot and stick; Peter Lush has been patient and competent; Mike Gatting, although he has not got everything right, has set a genial, positive lead, with the canny and thoughtful Emburey and the admirably resilient Gower acting as important assistants.

So, a happy and successful tour. I suppose the two things have always gone hand in hand, but it has been a pleasure to see it happen. At the end of each Test series I find it an interesting and usually also an informative exercise to nominate the best composite side. The XI to play on current form might be: Broad, Marsh, Jones, Border (captain), Gower, Botham, Richards, Emburey, Edmonds, Dilley and Reid. Waugh, Small and especially Gatting would be the most unfortunate to be omitted. 'Australeng' might beat the West Indies at Sydney, but not in many other places.

C.M-J.

The days when the end of an Ashes series meant the end of the tour in Australia are a thing of the past. Ahead now lay a month of One-Day Internationals for the grandiosely titled 'World Series Cup'. The weekend after the Sydney Test had England playing on two consecutive very hot days in Brisbane. They had a good win over the West Indies on Saturday and a narrow defeat by Australia on Sunday. Under the floodlights of Melbourne and Sydney during the week the West Indies beat Australia to square up matters and then England, or rather Allan Lamb, pulled the fat out of the fire in the last over against Australia. Lamb started the over needing to score 18 off six balls from Bruce Reid. He did it in five. The show rolled on to the Australia Day weekend in Adelaide . . .

Friday 23 January, Adelaide If it's Saturday, it must be the West Indies: this time in Adelaide where it is only slightly cooler than it was in Brisbane last Saturday when England agreeably surprised their supporters and disagreeably stunned the West Indies by bowling so well on a pitch which was helpful early on. Thus they sowed the seeds of a comfortable victory, their second in two matches against the side who could have beaten them in their sleep this time last year.

So well are England playing on this tour and so remarkably did they win last night despite *not* really playing very well, that it is tempting to think that they can go on winning no matter how well their opponents play. Last night's astonishing – one might almost say freak – burst of scoring by Allan Lamb, when the match had by all normal rules been won by Australia, was a case of nightlight robbery.

England will have to be steadier in the field, though – they were a bit careless at times yesterday – but Bill Athey's pieces of poaching at mid-wicket reprieved them.

Any changes are likely to be within the team rather than from without: in 'the team' I include Gladstone Small, who could come back for either Edmonds or DeFreitas. For the forgotten four I'm afraid the only hope of a game now may be if England qualify for the finals with games in hand. The longer they go without match practice, the harder it is to justify their inclusion for vital matches. French, Foster, Slack and Whitaker are caught in a vicious circle for which no amount of four-star hotels and sunny days can compensate. Rather like, I suppose, being well-qualified, eager to work, but unemployed.

C.M-J.

The pattern of the first few matches continued in Adelaide as England beat the West Indies, the West Indies beat Australia and Australia beat England. It was time for Christopher to make his last entry in his log . . .

Tuesday 27 January, Adelaide England are spending the day in Adelaide – many of the players on the golf course – reflecting ruefully on the fact that they should by now have been in a position from which neither the West Indies nor Australia could overtake them on points on the World Series Cup. Not the least disappointed members of the touring party are the unfortunate four, Foster, French, Slack and Whitaker, who could then have expected at least one match and possibly two of England's last three qualifying games.

It is absurd but true that England have won twice in this competition against potentially the strongest side yet have lost twice, and only avoided three defeats out of three by a miracle, against the weakest team. The failures against Australia stem from England's inability to deal with Peter Taylor's tidy, looping off-spin and the failure also of the big four, Gatting, Gower, Lamb and Botham, to produce the volume of runs they should. Lamb is in the best form and Gower always scores quickly and unselfishly, but Botham's one-day record for England is a poor one over a long period. This time he has bowled more sensibly than he has batted.

Tired though they are, I am sure England's discipline and spirit will carry them through to the finals and, very possibly, to the trophy which would give them a clean sweep of the spoils on offer in Australia this season.

I shall not be there to see them do it, as I must return to England after three months away. I remain strongly opposed to Australia's shortsighted exploitation of the One-Day International. The matches remain fashionable for young spectators, many of them, as one Perth judge succinctly put it, 'turning our cricket grounds into a larrikins' picnic'. Three tired teams playing each other eight times in order to eliminate one of the three is a clear overkill which undermines Test and Sheffield Shield cricket. To play each other twice would be quite sufficient and less numbingly monotonous for players and spectators.

C.M-J.

England now began to look the tired team they undoubtedly were, carrying injuries which hampered them in the field and losing both to Australia and the West Indies. One pleasant change was the inclusion of one of those 'forgotten four' – Neil Foster – in the side. Their presence in the finals hinged on defeating the West Indies in the Northern Tasmanian town of Devonport.

They set the West Indies only 178 to win and many gave them no further chance. But yet again the professionalism of the England bowlers put a stranglehold on the West Indies. None of the five of them went for more than three and a half an over which was just under the asking rate for the innings. England won by 29 runs.

Our reporting of the last few matches after Christopher's departure was in the hands of Henry Blofeld and Jack Bannister. Henry had been enjoying the adulation of the Australian public, laying on the 'archetypal Pom' act with a trowel and this time doing a great deal of ball-by-ball radio commentary for the Australian commercial network. His reporting position for that Devonport match, though, was not so glamourous: a lavatory at the back of the stand. For Jack, on tour for the Birmingham Post, the experience of radio reporting was a new one which he tackled with his customary thoroughness and professionalism, reacting positively to suggestions on style. Experienced as an expert summariser, the win in Devonport now presented him with a new challenge. He would be joining the ABC team as our man giving the ball-by-ball description of the finals which we would now be broadcasting.

When you've sat behind a *Test Match Special* microphone for 13 five-day Tests, safely cocooned in the protective warmth of a summariser's chair, the offer of moving three feet to starboard ought not to be regarded as a step into the completely unknown. After all, a mike is a mike, and a cricket match is still only a cricket match, and no more people are tuned in to one mike than the other, and . . .

Except that as a so-called expert, you speak when you, or your commentator, wishes, and not until then. The demands of a continuous thread of verbal description are not made, and the time-span of a Test match over – from four to seven minutes – can be used to collect, polish, and finally deliver the most erudite-sounding opinion. The biggest plus of the summariser's job is that, like polite and obedient children, you don't speak until you are spoken to.

So, having had the call, you ease your way through your first few Tests until, as confidence grows, your approach changes. The ego starts to expand and the first danger to avoid is offering repetitious or unnecessary opinion which, by definition, becomes 'inexpert'. You have probably arranged for your first offerings to be taped, and after the match, you go back and replay all those analyses you hope will seem as sound in retrospect as you thought they did at the time.

If the telephone rings the following season, then at least you can convince yourself that you must have impressed someone: until comes the enquiry which sounds casual but, with hindsight, is like a dagger into the ribs.

'How would you like a stab at commentating?' Gulp, pause, gulp again and you hear a ventriloquial voice off nonchalantly say, 'I'd love to'.

'Oh no you wouldn't', says the inner Doubting Thomas. 'Oh yes I would', says the whistler in the dark, who cannot believe that, like a distant dental appointment, Melbourne and Sydney, February 1987, will ever actually materialise.

Except that it does and, having bidden Christopher Martin-Jenkins an affectionate farewell in Adelaide – well perhaps not that affectionate since on the morning of his flight back to the UK he relieved me of 20 Australian dollars on the Royal Adelaide golf course – J.D. Bannister entered the magnificently-appointed media box in the MCG like a rabbit charging the headlights.

New boys at school? New MPs at Westminster? No comparison, because at least they have time to find their feet. I faltered into the ABC box to find the Australian *modus operandi* is much less homely and friendly than *TMS*. No 'Johnners', or 'Blowers', or 'the Alderman' or Fred or Trevor – or even dear old 'Mushy'! No letters or cakes, but plenty of chewing gum and cold drinks. No lurking Peter Baxter wandering around, apparently muttering to himself (you eventually realise he is talking back to base). No written order of microphone work but, instead, a bunch of friendly, but seemingly hard-bitten Antipodean types, all of whom, like policemen and travelling English cricket reporters, seem to get younger each tour.

'Hi Jacko – believe you're doing a spell.'

'Er, yes.'

'Fine. Don't hold back. Give it plenty of oomph – and never understate.'

Oh great. Not only do you have to find out whether or not you can swim in the deep end without flippers and arm bands, but you also have to do the butterfly when you were going to make do with a quiet and slow dog-paddle. So you talk to yourself to try and dispel that 'what *am* I doing here?' sinking feeling. 'Come on Banners. Bet Johnners isn't even awake, never mind listening. Let's look for a bit of good old English comfort.'

A sideways glance through glass to the next box, but that doesn't help, because there is Blowers galloping along at 150 miles an hour, with vibrating right leg keeping time as he confides his innermost thoughts – well nearly innermost – to one of his commercial fan clubs. Now you feel worse. Never mind, safety first. Play it straight – nothing fancy and no frills. Remember to give the wickets before the runs (i.e. after one wicket goes for ten runs, in England it is 10 for 1 but Down Under it has to be 1 for 10). Now you get the silly thought that you hope it is 1 for 1 so you can't get it wrong. The brain tells the voice, 'Don't get smart, and above all, no picking out any *double entendres* – particularly the unwitting ones'.

You're on. It's your turn, and suddenly all those blasted green and gold Australian pyjama outfits seem to have made individual identification impossible. Even Allan Border and Bruce Reid – 14 inches different in height – look the same. No matter, there's a wicket. Thank heaven. Bring in your summariser, to whom you give all of seven seconds to collect his thoughts. 'Dave Renneberg, David Gower has just been bowled. How did you see the dismissal?'

The taciturn Renneberg (oh where were you, F.S., when I needed you most?), tossed down his usual economic delivery. 'Not much footwork – in fact I would've felt much happier if David had got his leg over quicker.'

Every instinct screamed at me 'Recite the alphabet!' but no. The rabbit hit the headlights at full speed. 'Wouldn't we all?' I hear myself uttering to ill-concealed guffaws from the back of the box.

But, magically, the ice has been broken. You find to your great surprise and relief that talking throughout a six-ball over is not impossible, and you are through stage one.

The names come and go – Jim Maxwell, Jack Potter, Graham Dawson, Alan Hurst, Norman O'Neill, yet surprisingly you find you can remember to give English listeners the shape of commentary they are more conditioned to receiving. After all, life *is* different, when you are perched up in the roof of the Sydney Cricket Ground, with the downward-sloping stand roof blocking out the far sky-line. Even the eagle eye of Blowers would struggle to find a double-decker bus with 84 pigeons perched on it. Although perhaps not, knowing Henry.

So, full of courage, you dare to forecast an England win, only to find that is one vote out of seven, and again you wonder why you ever agreed to swap mikes and ask questions instead of answering them. But, in both Melbourne and Sydney, your one vote is a winner, and England do not have to face a third final.

Fire off a piece for Radio 2 news, Radio 4, Breakfast television and the World Service and the rest of the night is yours. Except that it is midnight and you still haven't eaten. Suddenly the lean and hungry look of yon C.M-J. is explained. Is anyone at home still speaking to you? Has the Gower 'leg-over' comment jammed the switchboard? Will you ever be allowed back into England? Yes, No, and Yes were the short answers – perhaps because everyone had switched you off by then.

And at the end of that first dip into the deep end? It was quite invigorating in a masochistic way. Extremely enlightening, and you find you are left with a keen wish to dive in again. After all, you and England have a 100 per cent winning record behind the commentating mike – leg-over or not.

J.B.

SUMMARISED SCORES

First Test at Brisbane : England won by 7 wickets
England	456 (Botham 138; Athey 76; Gatting 61; Gower 51)
and	77 for 3
Australia	248 (Marsh 56; G.R.J. Matthews 56 n o; Dilley 5-68)
and	282 (Marsh 110; Emburey 5-80)

Second Test at Perth : Drawn
England	592 for 8 dec. (Broad 162; Gower 136; Richards 133; Athey 96; Reid 4-115)
and	199 for 8 dec. (Gatting 70; Waugh 5-69)
Australia	401 (Border 125; Waugh 71; Dilley 4-79)
and	197 for 4 (Jones 69)

Third Test at Adelaide : Drawn
Australia	514 for 5 dec. (Boon 103; Jones 93; Waugh 79 n o; G.R.J. Matthews 73 n o; Border 70)
and	201 for 3 dec. (Border 100 n o)
England	455 (Broad 116; Gatting 100; Athey 55; Reid 4-64; Sleep 4-132)
and	39 for 2

Fourth Test at Melbourne : England won by an innings and 14 runs
Australia	141 (Jones 59; Botham 5-41; Small 5-48)
and	194 (Marsh 60)
England	349 (Broad 112; Reid 4-78; McDermott 4-83)

Fifth Test at Sydney : Australia won by 55 runs
Australia	343 (Jones 184 n o; Small 5-75)
and	251 (Waugh 73; Emburey 7-78)
England	275 (Gower 72; Emburey 69; Taylor 6-78)
and	264 (Gatting 96; Sleep 5-72)

Traveller's Tales

Don Mosey

As England continued their winter campaign on the great island continent, another member of the Test Match Special *team was in Australasia: the Baron von Munchausen of the commentary box. Except that – he assures us – his tales are true . . .*

Marooning a houseboat party on a mudbank in the Hawkesbury River of New South Wales would not be everyone's idea of the perfect mid-winter break in the sun. Nor does the experience of having a camper van blow up on you on the Canterbury Plains at five o'clock on a New Zealand Sunday afternoon have a general appeal to the average holiday-maker.

So it requires someone of a curiously perverse nature to say that two such disasters contributed to the enjoyment of his close-season travels in the winter of 1986–87. Such a perverse nature could really only be found in a Yorkshireman. After all, when one's little treasure-house of memories includes being tear-gassed in Lahore, getting hoofed out of Guyana as a member of a politically undesirable touring party and taking a ride in a Bombay taxi, most other experiences are bound to be an improvement.

January 1987 found me in Sydney, trying to survive the shock of watching the worst team in Australian cricket history beating England in the course of an otherwise virtually unblemished tour. It was a bonus of great magnitude to find the Opera House staging something other than a tuneless modern composition and offering instead the melodic delights of *The Mikado*. Being something of a traditionalist, I could not really approve of a chorus of gentleman of Japan opening Act I by parading around with brief cases and furled umbrellas, but this set-back was nothing compared with the entrance of Nanki Poo in the person of Mr Peter Cousins. My only previous experience of this young man was seeing him on television in a serial called *Return to Eden* in which he played the spoiled and feckless son of a wealthy family who spent the whole series perpetrating one disaster after another – a non-singing role which, I reflected as I left the Opera House, was a better piece of casting than presenting him as the incognito heir to the Emperor of Japan.

I have never shared the affection some of my colleagues – notably Henry Blofeld – cherish for Australia. The sun is too harsh for my delicate complexion for one thing; the ever-present dread of encountering a tiger snake or a funnel-web spider, whether I am on the outskirts of Dubbo or walking down Pitt Street, Sydney, is another. Indeed, one of my Australian friends (and strangely enough in view of this narrative I do have one or two) has dined out for years on the story of me stripping down the bed to search for reptilian or entomological intruders in a room 34 floors up in the Park Regis Hotel on my first visit to his fair city.

Thus it came as a great shock when my younger son, embarking on a round-the-world trip to see what he wanted to do with his life after emerging from Loughborough College of Physical Education with no vocation for teaching, decided it was unnecessary for him to proceed beyond Sydney. It came as an even greater shock when he forsook rugby for fishing but, blood being thicker than Toohey's (or even Resch's) bitter, it was clearly important to provide the little lad with a special treat for his 32nd birthday on 30 January. What better than a fishing trip to the Hawkesbury?

For two days we explored the complex reaches of that noble stream while fish of every shape, size and hue disported themselves about us., They leaped and cavorted on all sides, consumed vast quantities of prawns dangled over the side in temptation without ever considering for one moment swallowing the hook as well. Antipodean contempt for Pommie ineptitude reached its highest point for 48 long hours – literally so because small son, driven to a frenzy of fury by his failure to impress the aged parents, fished all night as well as all day. The ultimate humilation came on Saturday evening when his lady mother, reluctantly and gingerly holding a rod which had been prepared for her, hauled in a prize specimen on the first occasion in her life on which she had cast a line!

We cruised on, the birthday celebrations on a slightly more subdued note. Sunday night saw the good ship Pamela heading for a sheltered anchorage within reasonable striking distance from the base to which the houseboat had to be returned by 9.00 a.m. Progress became a trifle laboured which, in my nautical ignorance, I attributed to heading into the river's mainstream at low tide. Low tide it was indeed but that was the full extent of my navigational accuracy. We were, in fact, crawling along the bottom of a shallow reach, tangled with weeds, which in due course brought us to a grinding halt accompanied by a frenzied scream from the engine's overheating-warning system. A mile away, in the deep-water channel we should have been following, craft of all kinds sailed serenely to and fro. Half a mile away, on the near shore, a family frolicked on a sandy beach, unaware of the Pommie panic which was beginning to set in amid the mud and the weeds.

A quick scan of the instructions brought no comfort. 'If you have a complete breakdown, telephone back to base for assistance.' Telephone? One glance at the forested terrain suggested that if one of us swam/waded ashore, our chances of finding a telephone were about as remote as those of England in a Test against West Indies.

Another check on the instructions: 'If you run aground, lift the outboard so that it does not become embedded in the mud'. Small son, now beginning to enjoy himself for the first time since Mother's success with rod and line, jumped overboard, hoisted the motor into a horizontal plane and somehow we lashed it into position with a rope. 'Don't worry, Dad', he grinned, 'Everything will work out.' It had not taken him long to work up an easy-going Australian philosophy. Don't worry indeed! If we did not get off the mudbank soon it would be dark. We were not allowed to cruise in the dark. If we didn't get closer to base we would be late returning the boat the next day. We would then be late returning the hire-car in Sydney. And all this would result in our missing the 2.00 p.m. 'plane to New Zealand. Our friends waiting to greet us would have no idea where we were and ahead of us stretched an endless chain of cancelled arrangements. Don't worry, indeed!

A search of the cabin revealed a three-day-old newspaper giving high and low tide times at Sydney and Newcastle. An estimate somewhere between the two suggested that we had a minimum of three hours to wait before there was any hope of help from that quarter. We settled down, anxious parents, small son and his girlfriend Barbara, to play Scrabble in a manner which might have impressed Francis Drake, awaiting the arrival of the Armada, but which was by no means an indication of genuine *sang-froid*. Every ten minutes I took depth-soundings with a mop-handle; every 15 minutes I enquired, 'Do you think we should try to move yet?'

Three hours began to seem like three weeks as I thought of penalty clauses for the late returning of boats and cars. And then, with agonising slowness, the slap of the waves on the hull began to sound a little more vigorous; almost imperceptibly we began to swing around the anchor-chain. Four hours after we had run aground we slipped off the mudbank and, scarcely daring to look at the chart I had so asininely ignored four hours earlier, we began to inch our way across to the deep-water channel. It was pitch dark. Passing fishing boats, signalled to us in wild alarm. Antipodean oaths rent the night air. I ignored them all. The wrath of the entire maritime population of New South Wales was as nothing to a Yorkshireman compared with the horrors of paying extra fees for the late return of a boat and a car.

Somehow we groped our way through the darkness to an anchorage. Sleeping crews of sleek yachts leaped out in alarm as Pamela grunted and creaked her cumbersome way amongst the streamlined, ocean-going hulls. Advice and/or warnings and/or threats rang out from all sides. I pretended I could not hear them. The anchor rumbled overboard and we were safe for the night. My dreams during the next seven hours ranged from the wreck of the Titanic to the troubles of the Ancient Mariner. But at 6.00 a.m. the intrepid quartet were swabbing the decks in an attempt to destroy the evidence of the previous night's muddy adventures and before our neighbours had time to wake with recriminations we rumbled away back to base. At the wheel, I was once more monarch of all the estuary I surveyed as we sailed confidently into dock.

'The Sun came up upon the left,
Out of the sea came he!
And he shone bright, and on the right
Went down into the sea.'

Pamela was returned on time: 'G'dye. Had a good trip?' 'Sure, marvellous, thank you very much.'

The car was returned on time: 'G'dye. Enjoyed yourselves?' 'Absolutely splendid, thank you.'

The 'plane left on time and arrived in Auckland on time. Had I learned my lesson? Not on your life. Four days later I hired a camper van for a fortnight's tour of North and South Island.

'Just watch the oil', said the chap at the camper van depot.

'There shouldn't be any problem but if you are planning to go through the mountains it's as well to top up the oil every day, just in case.'

Every morning for the next eight days I religiously topped up the oil. After a quick dash across North Island we crossed the mill pond of the Cook Strait, relishing the delights of drinking gin and tonic at 8.00 a.m. as the ferry crept smoothly into Marlborough Sound and through the breathtaking beauty of the northern archipelago to the terminal at Picton. Away we went to bask in the sunshine of Nelson and plough through the rainstorms of the West Coast. Recalling a memorable broadcast by my colleague Chris Rea during a British Lions tour of the 1970s in which he described a wet Saturday in Westport, I sent him a postcard of the Cape Foulwind cement works (not the best pictorial advertisement for the delights of New Zealand) with the message that it was still raining in those parts.

We inspected glaciers and rain forests, climbed over dizzy passes through the Southern Alps, looked at the reflection of the snow-tipped mountains in jade-green lakes and every morning I religiously topped up the oil . . . It was probably the decision to make the long hop from Lake Wanaka to Christchurch in one day's drive which brought about our undoing, for 12 miles beyond the plains town of Geraldine the camper van ground to a halt. An inspection revealed that the oil had been leaking copiously throughout our day's travels. It was five o'clock on a Sunday afternoon, a point of the week in New Zealand which makes meditation in a Trappist monastery seem positively riotous.

Andrew and Barbara flagged down a (remarkably) passing car and returned to Geraldine in search of help. An hour later they returned in a pick-up driven by a young man who had, it transpired, been in the process of losing heavily to his mother-in-law in a poker game and was glad of the diversion. He towed us back into town, inspected the innards of the camper van and pronounced it totally knackered. Philosophically, we booked into the local pub, had a meal and went to bed. Tomorrow was another day.

At 9.00 a.m. the following morning we presented ourselves at the garage to find the staff had been on the 'phone to just about everyone in New Zealand who *might* be able to help (including the firm from whom we had hired the camper, 1,000 miles away in Auckland). Sadly, they had no alternative vehicle within 300 miles and all they could suggest was that we try to make our way back (1,000 miles!) and they would compensate us for our troubles. The First Test between New Zealand and West Indies was five days away and I did not rate my chances of joining the Radio NZ commentary team very highly. Andrew and Barbara were due to fly from Auckland back to Sydney in four days' time and I suggested they explore the possibilities of taking out New Zealand citizenship. As it all looked like being rather expensive, I walked down Geraldine's main street to the bank.

Returning miserably to the garage I found myself in conversation with one Don Stenhouse, local manager for the Mount Cook transport and travel combine. 'Don't worry', he said (now where had I heard that before?) 'Don't worry; there's no problem. You want to get to Christchurch first of all, right? Just take my car and leave it there. Someone will be going through during the week and I'll arrange for it to be picked up. Now, I'm sure the ladies would like to freshen up. I've 'phoned my wife and she'll give you a spot of lunch while we 'phone Auckland and see if your camper van people have been able to sort something out for you.'

Can anyone imagine that happening anywhere else on earth – lending one's car to a group of total strangers and trusting them to deliver it, intact to a city over 100 miles away? It was, let me say at once, a characteristic example of New Zealand kindness and hospitality – absolutely typical. As we climbed into Don Stenhouse's brand new Ford Laser, alongside the accumulated camper-vanning gear of a fortnight, small son whispered in my ear, 'Now I know why you think these people are the best you have ever met'.

My Auckland contacts were still unable to provide a substitute vehicle when we telephoned them from Christchurch. They were overcome with remorse (and, let me add, gave us a rebate of 1,400 dollars on an original outlay of 1,600 when we ultimately reached Auckland, although we had already had eight days of enjoyment from the camper van when it conked out), but could we possibly get ourselves back to North Island? We could, and did – in a Honda City, which is roughly the size of a Mini, and we still had the accumulated camper-vanning gear for four people for a fortnight! It was the last car available for hire in Christchurch on the basis of a one-way trip to Auckland. The chap who fixed us up was the son of Tom Burtt, the slow left-arm bowler who toured England in 1949 and who took the wicket of my friend, Brian Close, for nought in Closey's first Test Match. Small world. I reached Wellington in time for the First Test versus West Indies; the kids reached Auckland in time for their 'plane to Australia; my wife reached a hairdresser in time to prevent her hair turning completely white and extracted from me, when we met up for the Second Test in Auckland, a solemn promise never, never again to embark upon ambitious holidays in unfamiliar transport.

For the winter of 1987–88 I am considering pony-trekking in Colorado.

The 1987 Commentators

Trevor Bailey

In the early months of each year, when the coming of spring is still more a hope than an expectation, a very small committee meets in Broadcasting House to choose the commentary teams for the summer's Test Match Specials. It takes more agonising discussion than you might think and often some compromise, but eventually a list is drawn up and each member of the team can be told of his appointed duties for the season ahead.

One letter always goes to Trevor Bailey's house in 'The Drive'. (Is that, I wonder, the stroke you would remember him by?) His clipped assessment of players and situations ('Good ball – bad shot', or 'Nice little player – like him in my side') have earned Trevor the nickname, 'Mr Jingle'. Sometimes his predictions, made with such certainty, come a little unstuck. Who can forget the first World Cup final? 'The game is basically over. Australia would have been pushed to make 220; they will no more make 250 than go fly a kite.' They made 274 and fell only 17 runs short of the West Indies. But one tends to forget the many times when the predictions are right and no one enjoys the joke more than Trevor when they go wrong. He is a tremendously loyal member of the commentary team, constantly concerned about the programme. He seemed the ideal man to run the rule over his colleagues for the season.

My commanding officer, Colonel Peter Baxter, BBC and numerous Bars throughout the world, wished me luck without too much conviction. He added those immortal words so beloved of army officers: 'We are depending upon you', despite knowing that he was sending me on an impossible mission.

My assignment was a tough one: to conquer the West Indies under the command of Clive Lloyd. The stakes were high – the future fate of *TMS* hung in the balance. If I failed, Radio 3 would be devoted entirely to classical music, Derek Jameson giving elocution lessons and Pam Ayres reading poetry. The task became even more formidable when the Colonel gave me my troops in batting order. The days when this was decided by the captain have long since passed, and it is now the responsibility of the manager, technical manager, coach, physiotherapist, psychologist, seven minders and three public relations officers. The last three also give a press conference before the toss, after the toss, at the fall of each wicket, during each interval and at stumps.

The class of '87: front row: Christopher Martin-Jenkins, Trevor Bailey, Brian Johnston and Mushtaq Mohammed; back row: Peter Baxter, Henry Blofeld, Robin Jackman, Jack Bannister, Bill Frindall and Don Mosey.

How would my XI fare against the might of the West Indies? Apart from the obvious language difficulties, which might possibly cause a walkout, though never a run-out, I was not worried about my experienced pair of openers, Milburn and Blofeld. I had seen both in action in many parts of the globe opening bottles with a skill and alacrity that would have satisfied even parched Aussies.

Colin, an expert on nightclubs, could be relied upon to undermine some of the opposition's stamina, while his rendering of 'Love on the Rocks' was a certain recipe for indigestion. Any innings by Henry could be relied upon to contain at least 20 buses of various hues and destinations, including several good-looking ones. There would also be a perpetual flow of aeroplanes, several happy helicopters and a nice line in trains, although there is no truth in the rumour that he is about to be appointed public relations officer to the Ministry of Transport. Other ingredients he could be depended upon to provide included butterflies, thoughtful pigeons and a seemingly endless supply of exotic birds.

The problem about my number three, Christopher Martin-Jenkins, was not his elegant style, but whether he would arrive. Not for nothing is he known as the late cricket correspondent of the BBC, as well as Rory Bremner's impressionist coach.

Mushtaq Mohammad might be termed an original oriental mystery, made the more baffling by his Birmingham background, and one which I would not fancy the opposition to solve easily. They could also have trouble dealing with his curry cake.

The Long Room is now normally regarded as the Squire of St John's Wood's personal lounge. Squire Johnston has never failed to provide a vast collection of goodies: cakes, sweets, wine, odd noises and pre-music-hall puns and jokes. In addition to his batting, Johnners has acquired a reputation behind the timbers, which meant that I would have to position my fine leg so fine that he was immediately behind the Squire.

The presence of Sir Frederick Trueman guaranteed that there would at least be plenty of line and length from one end, plus a good cabaret turn. He would also be an asset in the friendly golf match arranged for the Sunday, because there are fewer more feared bush rangers to be found roaming the courses of the world picking up prizes. There once was a time when Fred was surprised when he won a competition, now he is amazed if he has not. It must, however, be admitted that over the years he has been very shrewd in arranging the composition of his team.

Another formidable golf player with the same Northern determination to win is the Alderman. Don is a lover of cricket and rugby with a fine command of the English language, but his choice of music and singers does not include Boy George and Madonna. The big mystery is why, with a larger vocabulary, he is consistently beaten by the Squire at the Word Game. The answer is that the Squire, like so many successful batsmen, has learned to play within his limitations, while the Alderman probably has too many strokes.

Robin Jackman, known as the 'Shoreditch Sparrow' on account of his high-pitched, usually optimistic and excrutiatingly loud appeals, will go down in history as the first man to stop (for a time) an entire tour without bowling a ball. This made him immensely popular with his colleagues in the England team who considered the best part of Guyana to be the departure lounge at the airport.

West Indians love to gamble, and Jack Bannister is always prepared to accept bets on anything, which is bound to make him very popular initially. However, he is a very shrewd operator, and by the end of the match the one certainty is that Jack, like any natural bookie, will end up on the winning side. For once, I find this most encouraging, unlike on those occasions I have had wagers with him.

The BBC selection committee had obviously been impressed by the success enjoyed by the West Indies over the past decade with their quartet of pacemen, so they went one better by picking six seamers. This meant that I was entrusted with an attack even more unbalanced than the one Peter May gave to David Gower in his first outing as captain at Lord's against Pakistan. That had consisted of four right-arm seamers between fast and fast-medium – Ian Botham, Robin Jackman, Ian Greig and Derek Pringle – plus an off-spinner, Eddie Hemmings, of just under medium pace. So although David was able to change his bowlers, he could not alter his bowling. To make matters worse for me, this heavy emphasis on seam meant that my batting line-up was somewhat lacking in depth, class, strokes and ability.

The outlook was grim. How could I avoid yet another massive West Indian victory and the end of *TMS*? It was then I remembered my secret weapon, my number 11. Bill is a natural number 11, unless you are lucky enough to be playing 12-a-side, or he happens to be the skipper. Although a genuine, 11-carat, next to the roller man, he could win me this match, because nobody, not Viv Richards, not Gordon Greenidge, has scored so many runs as The Bearded Wonder. Now complete, my selection looked like this:

1. Colin Milburn
2. Henry Blofeld
3. Christopher Martin-Jenkins
4. Mushtaq Mohammad
5. 2nd Lieutenant T.E. Bailey RM
6. Squire Brian Johnston
7. Sir Frederick Trueman of Flasby Manor
8. Alderman Don Mosey
9. Robin Jackman
10. Jack '10 to 1 the field' Bannister
11. Bill 'The Bearded One' Frindall

I was about to toss up with Viv Richards when Peter Baxter gave me a nudge, Brian a cake, Fred a cigar, The Alderman a glass, and I realised that I had, understandably, dropped off waiting for the Lord's caterers to bring our lunches before the tea interval.

60 Years of Cricket on the Air

Peter Baxter

Cricket Broadcasting was born on 14 May 1927. In 1987 BBC Radio Sport celebrated 60 years of commentary, starting with rugby in January and then soccer, the two sports which gave rise to the expression 'square one', when an announcer sitting beside the commentator used to identify the position of the action by calling out numbers which corresponded to a grid chart of the pitch printed in the *Radio Times*. Cricket, I felt, was worth a special look, as it had surely become the most successful sport on the radio. But I knew that it had not always been so. I decided to put on a programme during the One-Day Internationals which closely followed the anniversary to celebrate the diamond jubilee of cricket broadcasting.

I had always believed that Sir Pelham Warner had been the first cricket commentator, but Robert Hudson, himself both a former commentator and a Head of Outside Broadcasts, had dug up a document which showed that in fact the Rev Frank Gillingham, a former Essex batsman, had given the first live broadcast of cricket on Essex against the first New Zealand touring team at Leyton, then the county's headquarters. (Warner, however, did do the first broadcast from Lord's later that year.)

My early research took me to the BBC Reference Library and the old bound copies of the *Radio Times*. I found that the programme concerned had been one of waltzes and foxtrots interspersed with Gillingham's reports, or 'eye-witness accounts' as they were then described. To show that the BBC did appreciate that new ground was being broken by the live broadcasting of cricket, the *Radio Times* published a full-page article under the heading 'Cricket on the Hearth'. 'Broadcasting cricket', it said, 'is, of course, a new departure – an experiment, and something of an adventure. Cricket is one of the slowest games in the world. Obviously to broadcast a running commentary on a cricket match by the method used for Rugger Internationals, the Cup Final, the Boat Race or the Grand National would be impossible. What will be done is this. A microphone will be installed in the pavilion at Leyton, and the BBC's narrator will watch the whole of Saturday's play from there. At fixed times, beginning with the resumption of play after the lunch interval, and thereafter for a few minutes every hour, he will broadcast an account of the state of the game and after the close of play he will give a general description of the match. At other times, if anything happens worthy of special notice, his story will be "faded into" the afternoon programme from the studio that will be going on all the rest of the time.

'In this way, it is hoped, listeners will be given the gist – not to say the cream – of the match. They will not have to sit through descriptions of maiden overs and wait whilst the batsman sends in to the pavilion for his cap, but they will be able to listen every hour and hear the very latest score and any notable incidents of the last hour's play.'

I wonder what the author of that would make of today's *Test Match Special*. But even three years later a contributor to *The Listener* wrote, 'Arrangements have been made to broadcast eye-witness accounts of the five Test matches after the close of each day's play; and this reminds us again that first-class cricket does not lend itself to a good running commentary'.

Evidently there was more demand than had originally been foreseen, because by the final Test of that 1930 Ashes series, which saw the first appearance of Bradman in England, the *Radio Times* was cautiously promising a bit more than just a close of play 'eye-witness account', stating that it was 'hoped' to have lunch and tea interval reports as well; not over-generous when one considers that on one Test match Saturday that year there was scheduled live commentary on Wimbledon, the Hendon Air Display and the departure of the liner 'Britannic' on her maiden voyage.

In that 1930 article in *The Listener* which dismissed the idea of running commentary on first-class cricket it was suggested that village cricket might make a more entertaining subject. Sure enough, in the archives I found a recording of a commentary on a village match in Surrey, broadcast in 1938. The commentator was Tommy Woodroffe, later to acquire immortality with his 'fleet's lit up' broadcast. As a cricket commentary it left something to be desired, but it was highly amusing, particularly the sound effects of ducks quacking and a motorbike revving as the fast bowler ran in, not to mention the problems of giving the score because the small boy who was operating the scoreboard was not too keen on standing out in the rain.

I then embarked on a really enjoyable series of visits to reconstruct the development of radio cricket commentary. First I needed to find someone who knew Canon Gillingham well. As he had been an Essex man, I asked Trevor Bailey's advice. Without hesitation he recommended T.N. Pearce, captain of the county in the 1930s and '40s. I arranged to meet him at Arundel, where the Pakistan touring team were due to play the opening match of their campaign against Lavinia Duchess of Norfolk's XI. It was a thoroughly miserable day on the South Downs. The Castle Park was enveloped in mist and persistent drizzle and even the usually optimistic John Barclay – despite the undampable enthusiasm which has earned him the task of starting the cricket school at Arundel – was resigned to a washed-out day. So it was in his car that I found Tom Pearce, this legend of Essex cricket, who, although their careers had not quite overlapped, had indeed known Gillingham, whose Essex qualification, he suggested with a laugh, might have been that he was born in Tokyo and Essex was the nearest first-class county. He told me stories of this powerful character and fine batsman, his humour and the preaching which enabled him to fill his church in the City.

This, then, was the father of cricket broadcasting, who later was to dismay his BBC masters by filling in with a recital of the advertising hoardings round The Oval. But what had changed the Corporation's mind about the feasibility of running commentary on cricket? Robert Hudson had the answer for me. It was the arrival as Head of Outside Broadcasts of a tall, angular lawyer called Seymour de Lotbiniere, always known to his staff as 'Lobby'. He devised the way in which this commentary could be done and found the man to carry out his ideas in Howard Marshall. By the time Bradman paid his second visit to England with the 1934 Australians, BBC Radio was carrying spells of commentary. Indeed, the earliest commentary in the archives is of Hedley Verity's famous Test at Lord's in that series. Bob Hudson himself, as a commentator and later as Head of Outside Broadcasts, was a great believer in the form of commentary. He recalled what Wilfred Rhodes, whose sight had failed, had said to him: 'Paint a picture and keep it the right way up'.

E.W. Swanton, whom I visited in his delightful house in the furthest corner of Kent, had a special place in the story of commentary, having started before the War. He told me of his debut at a county match between Surrey and Lancashire at The Oval in August 1938, which he made as a trial before going to South Africa to cover the MCC tour of that winter. The Oval match had given Jim a harsh baptism. His morning spell of commentary consisted of a half-hour split evenly with Percy Fender, who was covering a match at Hove. Then Jim slipped away to attend the wedding of his old friend Henry Longhurst at Dulwich, having arranged to be brought up to date on his return by the captain, Monty Garland-Wells. This duly happened, but when he took up his position in a cubicle near the press box it was to hear this time from Percy Fender that rain had brought play to a halt at Hove and so he was on his own for half an hour. To make matters worse, he started when nine wickets were down and so shortly found himself having to fill the ten-minute interval between innings with no scorer or summariser to help him. 'Mind you,' said Jim, 'I'd had a glass of Champagne.' His efforts were rewarded and he found himself bringing live commentary to Britain from South Africa that winter, with the excitement of describing a hat-trick by Tom Goddard in his first Test and converting the South Africans to the possibilities of radio commentary.

On a glorious spring morning I drove through fresh, green Surrey woods to see Rex Alston. As always his voice and his appearance, too, belied his 86 years as indeed does his recent marriage. He and his bride of less than a year, Joan, were bubbling with enthusiasm. Rex told me how he joined the BBC as a wartime billeting officer. But he was soon doing a commentary trial and shortly after that the live description of a match at Abbeydale Park, Sheffield. For the Victory Tests, Rex found himself accompanying Howard Marshall, who was fresh from his role as a war correspondent after the allied invasion of Europe. When Marshall was recalled from Old Trafford to London for other events during the course of the match there, Rex was plunged in at the deep end.

The post-war euphoria for cricket was met by a new commentary team and an appetite for their descriptions. E.W. Swanton returned from the miseries of a Japanese prisoner-of-war camp to join forces with Rex Alston for those golden

Rex Alston (right) at the microphone in the
1950s.   S&G Press Agency

summers when the runs flowed again and huge crowds relished the deeds of Hammond, Hutton, Compton and Edrich. A new recruit was then brought into commentary from the unlikely source of the BBC's Eastern Service.

To talk to him I had to climb aboard a small yellow aeroplane which carried me from Southampton to the Channel Island of Alderney. John Arlott's welcome was as warm as ever. He gave me a guided tour of his delightful island home, and then we settled down over a glass of Muscadet to record the tale of how he had started as a cricket commentator.

In 1946 an Indian touring team came to England and the Head of the BBC's Eastern Service, fearing that the regular domestic commentators would make a hash of the Indian pronunciations, sent John to cover the first tour match at Worcester. The BBC man in Delhi immediately cabled Bush House in London to say what a success the broadcasts had been and to insist that they be continued. John had achieved his greatest ambition. 'For the others,' he said, 'it was no great translation, but I felt as if I had been turned upside-down.' The former Hampshire policeman was in seventh heaven.

So, when Bradman's powerful 1948 Australians arrived in England, the BBC had three commentators ready to describe the Test series, with A.E.R. Gilligan as the expert comments man. From the Australian Broadcasting Commission came a former New South Wales captain, who had started his broadcasting career before the War, when he was still playing: Alan McGilvray. For the first time a Test series in England was covered ball-by-ball – but not all of it for domestic consumption: Australians were listening as every ball was bowled. However, the start was a little uncertain. Rex Alston, the staff man organising as well as leading the commentary team, recalls the first morning of the series, when light rain delayed the start and they did not know whether to keep talking or to hand back to the studio. Eventually a plaintive voice in Rex's headphones begged him to hand back.

A taste was growing for radio cricket commentary, despite the brevity of the spells that listeners in Britain were allowed. The system of regional broadcasting that prevailed then carried periods of commentary on county matches, remembered now with great affection, but at the time they were sometimes frustratingly short. They were the ideal training ground for Test commentators and fuelled the public demand that made it apparent by the late 1950s that continuous Test match commentary was not only desirable but also the only way to avoid editorial anomalies in the coverage. In 1957, by incorporating the Third Network to join the Light Programme and Home Service (the forerunners of Radio 2 and 4), all-day commentary started under the title *Test Match Special* and carried the slogan: 'Don't miss a ball, we broadcast them all'. And what a match the new service had for its birth! The First Test of 1957 saw May and Cowdrey batting for hour after hour at Edgbaston to save England from the threat of Ramadhin and resurrect their hopes for the series against the West Indies.

The following year brought Robert Hudson's debut on *Test Match Special* and following him came Alan Gibson, Neil Durden-Smith and several more visitors from overseas: Charles Fortune from South Africa; Ken Ablack, Roy Lawrence and later Tony Cozier from the West Indies; Pearson Surita from India; Omar Qureishi from Pakistan and Alan Richards from New Zealand. But probably the biggest long-term impact on *Test Match Special's* personnel came in the mid '60s when the then Head of Outside Broadcasts, Charles Max-Muller, felt that the recently appointed BBC cricket correspondent should be doing radio commentary on Test matches as well as the television commentary he had been involved in since its re-start after the War. Brian Johnston has been the leading light ever since.

At the beginning of 1970 BBC Television policy was changed and B.J. was dropped. But the viewers' loss was the listeners' gain and Brian himself has often found in his journeys round the country that what people most enjoy in the programme is its friendliness. When he appointed me producer of *Test Match Special*, Robert Hudson counselled me that the programme was to many people 'company'; and from its origins, a simple description of a game of cricket, that is what it has become. The true triumph, surely, is in that great game itself.

England v Pakistan 1987

The First Test at Old Trafford

Fred Trueman

The One-Day Internationals always give us a very hectic 'net' for the Test Match Specials to follow. The commentary is given at a greater pace and although it is only for one day at a time, that day is longer, but the issue is somehow less serious than the 'real thing' of the Test cricket to come. This 1987 Texaco Trophy series gave several of our number the chance to see some of the Pakistan touring team for the first time and to wrestle with the problems of identification that they present almost uniquely with so many players of similar build and hairstyle. We were very grateful for Mushtaq Mohammed's presence to help us in this area.

The first match at The Oval was an easy enough win for England, and confirmed their winter form. Despite a century from Javed Miandad they overhauled Pakistan's 232 for 6 with only three wickets down and almost two overs in hand, Chris Broad making 99. Broad was again top scorer at Trent Bridge two days later with 52, but this time the tables were turned and Pakistan overcame a modest England total without too much trouble. So the series was poised for the decider at Edgbaston on Spring Bank Holiday Monday.

For the third time Javed Miandad was the top scorer for Pakistan, on this occasion with 68 out of 213 for 9. In reply England lost their eighth wicket at 167, but DeFreitas and Foster staged the heroics which saw them to the brink of victory before DeFreitas went for 33 and Greg Thomas joined Foster to see them home by one wicket with three balls to spare. It was breathtaking stuff as a curtain-raiser to the forthcoming Test series, but sadly the newspaper headlines next day concentrated on the crowd trouble in which a young man had his throat slashed by flying glass. We all left the ground hoping that this was no portent for the rest of the tour. In just over a week we would be meeting again in Manchester for the First Test . . .

It is not often that I turn up at a Test match full of schoolboy excitement, but the start of this new series aroused that feeling in me. Let me start the day before the match with the visit to Old Trafford of our old friend John Arlott, the great voice of radio cricket commentary. The Lancashire committee had had the happy idea of flying him over from Alderney to open the new 'Cardus Suite' at the Warwick Road end of the ground. This comprises an executive suite on the first floor with a splendid new press box above it, so they could have had no more fitting a person to open it and to pay tribute to Sir Neville Cardus, who reported on so many matches there for the *Manchester Guardian*.

This was the first time I had seen John since his last commentary at Lord's in 1980, so I was delighted to meet up with him again. In his speech John brought back great memories of Sir Neville and the marvellous service he gave to cricket writing and we all enjoyed just hearing that lovely, rolling Hampshire accent again. It was a speech to remember and a suitable preliminary to the First Test. Sadly, even as John spoke, the rain started to fall and it persisted all that afternoon and through the night. But there was an air of jollity in the Cardus Suite as, following John's speech, we toasted the 21st birthday of Lancashire's new signing, the Pakistan fast bowler Wasim Akram. A large part of his family had come over from Pakistan for the occasion and took up one table at the lunch. However, Bill Frindall put something of a damper on the occasion by revealing that this 21st birthday did not coincide with the one in the record books.

The England selectors had surprised everyone by not picking Tim Robinson to go to Australia the previous winter after a splendid season of county cricket for Nottinghamshire, but now he was back in the side. His county opening partner, Chris Broad, however, who had won all the honours in Australia, had had to withdraw with a broken finger. So it was Bill Athey, who had stood in as an opening batsman with success throughout the Australian tour, who was once again given that job with a new partner. This brought in the local hero, Neil Fairbrother, to bat in the middle order. Strange that an opening batsman should be replaced by a middle-order batsman, but that is something that we have come to expect over the years.

We arrived on the first morning to find a very damp Old Trafford and indeed no play was possible until mid-afternoon. At a table outside the main commentary box on our flat roof, exposed to the elements, sat Henry Blofeld, doing the news reports for Radio 2 and Radio 4 and envying us in our warm and comfortable box.

When play did start Pakistan won the toss and put England in although we were immediately surprised at this decision when Imran Khan, their main strike bowler, did not bowl himself. No explanation was forthcoming, but when the Pakistan manager, Haseeb Ahsan, was questioned about this in the press box he replied, 'Imran will bowl when Imran wants to bowl'. Haseeb was to make quite a reputation for himself on this tour and to provide journalists with something to write about on wet days.

In fact Imran did not bowl at all during the England innings and so Tim Robinson took his chance on a slowish wicket after Athey had been bowled off his pads. Robinson was 62 not out that night (and the next afternoon was to go on to make 166), but before that there was drama on that first evening when, in the last half-hour, Mike Gatting was out for 42 and young Neil Fairbrother came in to make his Test debut on his home ground. He got a warm welcome from the Lancashire members, although one or two wondered why he had not been given the protection of a nightwatchman. He didn't manage to put a bat to any of the four balls he received from Mohsin Kamal, padding up to the fourth, which would have knocked out the middle stump, so that the umpire had no hesitation in giving him out. So Neil Fairbrother did what so many great players have done before him: made nought in his first Test innings. There was a man called Graham Gooch who made a pair in his first Test, and Sir Leonard Hutton made nought and one, so he is in good company and my advice would be not to worry about it but to get his head down and carry on.

With Fairbrother out a nightwatchman did appear in the person of Bruce French, now providing that protection for the vastly more experienced David Gower. French more than did his job by going on the next morning to score his first half-century in Test cricket, and was a little upset at being out for 59 when he was just beginning to fancy his chances of making a hundred. Tim Robinson said later that as he watched some of the previously unsuspected strokes from his Nottinghamshire colleague, he thought he was batting at the other end from Wally Hammond.

With 22 from David Gower and 48 from Ian Botham, both of them, I feel, picked on past performances rather than current form, England got to the satisfying total of 447. But rain delays on the third day meant that the innings did not end before mid-afternoon. As we waited and talked ourselves dry on *Test Match Special* that Saturday morning, we saw a shot on the television monitor of the *Sport on 2* team, Henry Blofeld and Colin Milburn, outside in the wet huddled under an umbrella. I suggested that it was the kind of picture you would put on the mantlepiece to keep the kids away from the fire.

Relations between the two sides had unfortunately been given a poor start by events on the field the previous day. We had commented on the continuous comings and goings of the fielders and at one stage the England manager Micky Stewart had been seen on the dressing-room balcony with other England players apparently counting the Pakistan fielders to make sure they had no more than 11 on at any one time. It seemed to me on a visit to the pavilion that the touring team was about 20 strong now. The Saturday newspapers carried reports that Micky Stewart had accused the Pakistan fielders of deliberate time-wasting. This prompted a very sharp and critical reply from Haseeb Ahsan, who said in a statement that he did not wish this to mar the good relations between the two teams but it would have been better if Stewart had spoken to the officials of the touring team first. I felt it had all been taken a little out of context and blown up beyond belief, but this kind of constant coming and going must be curbed in the future.

Also off the field on the third day there was a bombshell for the England selectors – although it was not too much of a surprise to one or two in the know – when David Gower announced that he would be unavailable for the World Cup in India and Pakistan in autumn 1987 and for the tours of Pakistan, Australia and New Zealand which were to follow in another busy winter. It certainly did not surprise me, with the World Cup coming so soon after our season. This was also Gower's benefit year, and he had played ten years' international cricket, summer and winter, almost non-stop. The over-concentration on Tests and One-Day Internationals is causing

players to foresake their roots in county cricket.

Monday's play was limited to just under an hour and a half: a major disappointment for England, who had got themselves into a magnificent position with Pakistan 140 for 5, still nearly 300 runs behind with every chance of having to follow on. Ian Botham had snatched the prize wicket of Javed Miandad, but I noticed that his bowling would have to show a great improvement if there was not to be a large hole in England's attack.

In the event, the Manchester weather saved Pakistan. There was no more play after lunch on the fourth day, with the whole of the final day being washed out. I felt very sorry for the England team. They were riding the crest of a wave after their brilliant success in Australia, and they were right to be full of confidence even to the point of a little cockiness. There is nothing like confidence for breeding success and I do believe that if it had not been for the rain England would have started the series with a win, and that would have made a big difference to the series as a whole.

ENGLAND 1ST INNINGS v. PAKISTAN (1ST TEST) at OLD TRAFFORD, MANCHESTER on 4.5.6.8 JUNE 1987. TOSS: PAKISTAN

IN	OUT	MINS	No.	BATSMAN	HOW OUT	BOWLER	RUNS	WKT	TOTAL	6s	4s	BALLS	NOTES ON DISMISSAL
2.45	4.49	105	1	C.W.J. ATHEY	BOWLED	WASIM AKRAM	19	1	50	·	1	93	Off stump. Bowled through 'gate' via pad.
2.45	4.50	528	2	R.T. ROBINSON	C' SALIM YOUSUF	MOHSIN KAMAL	166	6	373	·	16	366	4th = TEST (1st in match) Its for ENG · PAK at Old Trafford. Edged hook
4.51	6.35	104	3	M.W. GATTING *	BOWLED	MOHSIN KAMAL	42	2	133	·	7	84	Off stump. Bowled through 'gate'.
6.37	6.40	3	4	N.H. FAIRBROTHER	LBW	MOHSIN KAMAL	0	3	133	·	·	4	TEST DEBUT. Padded up to break-back.
6.42	1.55	155	5	B.N. FRENCH †	C' IMRAN	WASIM AKRAM	59	4	246	·	10	112	(Night watchman) HS in TESTS. Drove to mid-off (high, 2 handed catch)
1.57	2.44	47	6	D.I. GOWER	C' SALIM YOUSUF	WASIM AKRAM	22	5	284	·	4	42	Top-edged pull - skier (keeper moved towards leg-slip)
2.47	5.14	127	7	I.T. BOTHAM	C' WASIM AKRAM	TAUSIF	48	7	397	1	5	69	Drove skier to straight boundary - well judged catch.
4.54	1.45	47	8	J.E. EMBUREY	C' SHOAIB	MOHSIN KAMAL	19	9	413	·	4	31	Square-drove hard to cover-point.
5.16	1.42	22	9	P.A.J. DeFREITAS	BOWLED	WASIM AKRAM	11	8	413	·	2	19	Played on to short delivery, just outside off stump.
1.44	2.20	36	10	N.A. FOSTER	BOWLED	TAUSIF	8	10	447	·	·	20	Deceived by flight.
1.46	(2.20)	34	11	P.H. EDMONDS	NOT OUT		23			1	3	30	
				* CAPTAIN † WICKET-KEEPER	EXTRAS	b 9 lb 15 w 1 nb 5	30						2s 5s 870 balls (inc 8 no balls)

UMPIRES: H.D. BIRD & B.J. MEYER
TOTAL (143.4 overs; 613 minutes) 447 ALL OUT at 2.20 pm on 3rd day.

14 OVERS 0 BALLS/HOUR
3·11 RUNS/OVER
51 RUNS/100 BALLS

BOWLER	O	M	R	W		HRS	OVERS	RUNS		RUNS	MINS	OVERS	LAST 50
WASIM AKRAM	46	11	111	4	3¼	1	17	32		50	103	29.3	103
MOHSIN KAMAL	39	4	127	4	2½	2	16	29		100	170	44.4	67
TAUSIF AHMED	21.4	4	52	2	·	3	13	44		150	250	61.5	30
MUDASSAR NAZAR	37	8	133	0	·	4	13	40		200	325	80.5	75
			24			5	14	44		250	377	92.4	52
						6	15	36		300	440	107.3	63
		143.4	27	447	10	7	14	58		350	507	122.0	67
						8	14	45		400	554	130.5	47
2ND NEW BALL taken at 12.44 pm 2nd day						9	11	59					
- ENGLAND 215-3 after 85 overs.						10	12	34					

TOSS at 2.15 pm. RAIN DELAYED START UNTIL 2.45 pm

TEA: 46-0 [25 OVERS / 36 MIN] ATHEY 16* (36') ROBINSON 29* (86')

STUMPS: 145-3 [59 OVERS / 238 MIN] (1ST DAY) ROBINSON 62* (218') FRENCH 6* (21')

LUNCH: 225-3 [89 OVERS / 359 MIN] ROBINSON 94* (365') FRENCH 51* (143')

TEA: 320-5 [116 OVERS / 477 MIN] ROBINSON 143* (477') BOTHAM 10* (63')

STUMPS: 402-7 [131.4 OVERS / 553 MIN] (2ND DAY) EMBUREY 14* (37') DeFREITAS 5* (5')

WKT	PARTNERSHIP		RUNS	MINS
1st	Athey	Robinson	50	105
2nd	Robinson	Gatting	83	104
3rd	Robinson	Fairbrother	0	3
4th	Robinson	French	113	155
5th	Robinson	Gower	38	47
6th	Robinson	Botham	89	104
7th	Botham	Emburey	24	20
8th	Emburey	DeFreitas	16	22
9th	Emburey	Foster	0	1
10th	Foster	Edmonds	34	34
			447	

COMPILED by BILL FRINDALL

PAKISTAN 1ST INNINGS — IN REPLY TO ENGLAND'S 447 ALL OUT

IN	OUT	MINS	No.	BATSMAN	HOW OUT	BOWLER	RUNS	WKT	TOTAL	6s	4s	BALLS	NOTES ON DISMISSAL
2.33	3.12	38	1	RAMIZ RAJA	C' EMBUREY	DeFREITAS	15	2	21	.	1	29	Square-leg – diving forward.
2.33	2.47	14	2	SHOAIB MOHD	C' FRENCH	FOSTER	0	1	9	.		7	Edged late outswinger
2.48	12.47	198	3	MANSOOR AKHTAR	C' FAIRBROTHER	EDMONDS	75	5	139	.	12	182	Edged on-drive at leg-break to short extra-cover.
3.14	4.56	77	4	JAVED MIANDAD	C' FRENCH	BOTHAM	21	3	74	.	2	65	Under-edged cut – keeper up to stumps.
4.57	11.40	26	5	SALIM MALIK	RUN OUT [DeFREITAS/FRENCH]		6	4	100	.		21	Attempted run to square-leg – sent back by Akhtar
11.41	(12.54)	73	6	IMRAN KHAN *	NOT OUT		10			.	.	73	
12.49	(12.54)	5	7	MUDASSAR NAZAR	NOT OUT		0			.		9	
			8	SALIM YOUSUF †									
			9	WASIM AKRAM	DID NOT BAT								
			10	TAUSIF AHMED									
			11	MOHSIN KAMAL									

* CAPTAIN † WICKET-KEEPER

EXTRAS: b 9 lb 2 w 1 nb 1 = 13   0s 15 386 balls (inc 2 no balls)

TOTAL (64 OVERS - 220 MINUTES) 140-5

17 OVERS 2 BALLS/HOUR
2.18 RUNS/OVER
36 RUNS/100 BALLS

BOWLER	O	M	R	W		HRS	OVERS	RUNS		RUNS	MINS	OVERS	LAST 50
FOSTER	15	3	34	1	.	1	15	30		50	84	21.5	84
DeFREITAS	12	4	36	1	#	2	18	44		100	143	38.3	59
BOTHAM	14	7	29	1	-/	3	16	51					
EMBUREY	16	3	28	0	-								
EDMONDS	7	5	2	1			11	1					
	64	22	140	5									

STUMPS: 93-3 (3RD DAY) [38 OVERS 157 MIN] AKHTAR 42* (121) MALIK 3* (11) [354 BEHIND]

LUNCH: 140-5 [64 OVERS 220 MIN] IMRAN 10* (73) MUDASSAR 0* (5) [307 BEHIND]

NO PLAY POSSIBLE AFTER LUNCH ON 4TH DAY

MATCH DRAWN

MATCH AWARD: R.T. ROBINSON
(Adjudicator: T.W. GRAVENEY)

WKT	PARTNERSHIP		RUNS	MINS
1st	Ramiz	Shoaib	9	14
2nd	Ramiz	Akhtar	12	23
3rd	Akhtar	Miandad	53	77
4th	Akhtar	Malik	26	26
5th	Akhtar	Imran	39	66
6th	Imran	Mudassar	1	5
			140	

COMPILED by BILL FRINDALL

The Second Test at Lord's

Henry Blofeld

It was an early start on the first morning of the Second Test match, for I had been selected to do the early morning piece from Lord's for the second edition of the *Today* programme on Radio 4 at 8.25 a.m. It had been pouring with rain when I went to bed and when I climbed into my car I was amazed to find that south-west London, at any rate, was basking under a cloudless sky, but in view of the rain which had fallen the morning newspapers were forecasting a delayed start to the match.

As I approached Lord's, I came to a halt before turning sharp right into Cavendish Avenue, which takes you down to the Nursery End car park entrance. While I was stationary the military figure of the new and charming secretary of MCC, Lt-Col John Stephenson, sailed past me on his bicycle like some ship-of-the-line in full rig. As he pedalled vigorously towards the ground it struck me that it was a happy omen for the day. It always takes a little time, even after 20 years, to persuade the guardians of the car park entrance that my pass does allow me to bring my car into the ground.

Once that opening skirmish had been completed, I found Len in his usual genial form on the back door of the pavilion and after picking up the key to the broadcasting boxes and nearly tripping over the chap who was delivering the day's supply of milk, I made the long climb to our box in the left-hand turret of the pavilion, pausing on the way to say good morning to Nancy, who presides over the kitchens like a most benevolent despot. She promised me scrambled eggs when I had finished. At 8.26 and 30 seconds I informed listeners that the groundstaff were working like beavers and that I was confident that play would start on time at 11.00 a.m. I also spoke highly of the secretary of MCC's ability on two wheels before taking up Nancy's offer of scrambled eggs and coffee.

It was well past nine o'clock when more of the *Test Match Special* team clocked in. Our producer, Peter Baxter, was first up the steps (two at a time), into our eyrie. He was slightly miffed, too, for he was afraid I had misled the public by anticipating a prompt start. I told him with some authority that I had detected an air of quiet confidence around the ground, although if the truth were known I had consulted no one. I did not let on, but I was a trifle concerned that I had got it wrong and I watched anxiously while the umpires, David Constant and Alan Whitehead, made their frequent journeys to and from the middle. To make matters worse it was beginning to cloud over. The Fates were kind to me, however, and before long Alan Curtis announced over the public address system that play would begin on time and my reputation as a crystal ball-gazer was much enhanced.

There is an atmosphere on the first morning of a Test match at Lord's which is unique. I have little doubt that if I was an Australian I would say the same thing about the Sydney Cricket Ground, but when I walked through the quiet corridors of the pavilion that morning I could not help but think of the best-ever description of Lord's pavilion made by C.L.R. James in arguably the best cricket book ever to have been written, *Beyond a Boundary*. He likens it to a cross between Mount Olympus and Canterbury Cathedral. This time, though, the ground was different for the New Mound Stand, paid for through the generosity of J. Paul Getty Junior, was gleaming in all its ocean-going newness, ready for business for the first time. It is by any standards an extraordinary structure and, with its 11 white pagodas at the top, it looks like a cross between a liner and a rather dashing mosque.

Now, at last, it was finished and had ceased to resemble a highly questionable building-site. When I arrived in the early morning sun and looked across at the stand from the gap between the Grandstand and the Warner Stand, I found it breathtaking. Those pagodas, looking like 11 extremely exciting dollops of white icecream, gave it even while it was still empty a character I had never guessed at. It became better still as the customers found their seats and almost perfect when I went across during the first day and to drink at one of the bars on the top deck under the pagodas. It is a notable addition to the ground.

But back to more practical matters. The Bearded Wonder arrived with the many tools of his trade packed into two or three holdalls. Now that he has become the cricket correspondent of the Sunday Something-or-other, the aura he has about him of the Commander-in-Chief of the Ruritanian Army is even stronger. I felt that the well-known snort, which marks a commentator's error or statement involving a dreadful *double entendre*, was in danger of changing from a noise of humorous and genial derision to a command to the firing-squad to take aim.

Johnners' co-respondent shoes, in an equal mixture of brown and white, which have, if anything, watched even more Test matches than he has himself, came tripping up the stairs giving strength to the rumour that he is 75 years young. The Boil was in sparkling form, full of his plans for capturing and captivating the subcontinent of India and Pakistan during the World Cup. In fact, it looked as if he and I were both going to tackle only India and we began to lay our plans for a chapter or two later in this book which by the end of this Test match we had distilled into 'With Blowers and The Boil in India'. Flick over the pages to see what it has eventually become. The Boil's administrative capabilities were to be seen at their best for already there was no one at Air India whom he did not know, most particularly a lady called Tina who proved time and again that she was able to perform miracles with airline timetables. A slight huffing and puffing then announced the arrival of Ollie Milburn, who was looking both fresh and eager which made us think that he must have had a quiet night and have gone to bed before three o'clock. The squad was completed by Jack Bannister, armed with his full array of technical equipment which allows him to keep his readers in Birmingham abreast of events in between spells as a summariser. Any time and motion man would take off his hat to Jack.

Mike Gatting won the toss after the umpires had to their eternal credit decided that play would start on time, and he put England in to bat. It was a fascinating first day's cricket until the weather intervened shortly before 6.00 p.m. when England were 231 for 4. The Pakistanis, under Imran Khan, were determined to win their first-ever Test series in England while Gatting's side was no less anxious to prove that their Australian summer had been no fluke. Imran had used himself most sparingly in the early county matches on the tour and came in for plenty of criticism as a result, but he had certainly kept himself fit and in practice. His opening spell now was an illustration of this. While Chris Broad continued in his good form of the winter, he had his anxious moments against Imran. On the other hand Tim Robinson, the hero of Old Trafford, failed. Bill Athey became the centre of attention with the most commanding innings he has played in a Test match as he went to his first Test hundred. The previous November in Perth Athey had been yorked by Bruce Reid when four short of a hundred in the Second Test of that series. I well remember thinking as he walked back to the pavilion then at the WACA ground that those last four runs he did not make might have a considerable effect on the rest of his career. Athey is a batsman who needs the confidence of his own success more than most, and I felt that a Test hundred, especially against Australia, would have done wonders for his confidence and made him a more authoritative batsman. But now he had put all that right in the best possible way, although it was ironic that after a bad Third Test at Headingley he was left out of the side for the remaining two matches. It was a measure of his character that after this disappointment he forced himself back into each of the three sides for the winter tours. On that first day at Lord's he and Gatting seemed to be taking the match away from Pakistan when Gatting was run out going for a second run which was never there.

One of the mysteries of the first part of the summer had been the whereabouts of Pakistan's leg-spinner, Abdul Qadir. He had been selected for the tour, but his wife was expecting another child and if reports could be believed she was thought to have been affected by evil spirits. Qadir wanted to stay with her in Lahore for as long as he could. Javed Miandad was also late in joining the party for he had a sick wife and had also been given permission to stay at home. It became increasingly clear as the First Test came and went that neither Imran, the captain, nor Haseeb Ahsan, Pakistan's talkative manager, (who began the tour by becoming everyone's favourite joke although by the end he had become a mild irritant to say the least), had not the foggiest idea of Abdul Qadir's whereabouts nor when he was coming. Bulletins about Qadir's progress were a feature of most days in early June.

Lord's was very wet on the Friday, and when I had again made my early dash to the ground I was hailed by John Stephenson, standing on the outfield under a stately umbrella, for he wanted to come up and have a word. After making the ascent he told me first that he thought the chances of play that day were so slender as to be negligible and that I would be doing potential spectators a service if I said so on the *Today* programme and saved them the journey. He also said that as a result of my revelation of his bicycling exploits the previous morning he and his secretary had been warding off Fleet Street who, to a man, wanted to come and photograph him on his bicycle. He pretended to be angry but I think he rather enjoyed it.

It was one of those days when we prattled on in the box about anything and everything. As usual in those circumstances Johnners was very funny, but the best part of it came when we had the honour of a visit from our old friend, His Highness the Maharajah of Baroda, known nowadays, since Mrs Gandhi abolished Maharajahs and all hereditary princes, as Fatesingh Gaekwad. He is also a former contributor to *TMS* for when Indian toured England in 1974 he was our Indian expert summariser. We had decided then that we would call him 'Prince' on the air and the appellation has stuck. It is always fun to see him and now when he poked his most distinguished face round the door of the commentary box we seized on him.

He was full of confidence that the World Cup in India and Pakistan was going to be a great success. He himself was a member of the organising committee and so he knew exactly what arrangements had been made to ensure that everything ran according to plan. When asked if he thought there was any danger that the South African issue would still cause problems, he was adamant that it would not, that common sense would prevail and that cricket would be the winner. During this visit to the box he took on another, more unexpected assignment: he found that he had been unanimously elected as special travel agent for the World Cup to Trevor Bailey and myself. He assured us that he would fix our hotels and flights between the venues and so during the weekend I took copies of our itineraries round to his house in Chelsea. As I write Trevor and I are looking forward to travelling round India by royal appointment, as it were, if not in a howdah on an elephant's back. Come to think of it, that might not be a bad way for The Boil and Blowers on what I am sure will be a triumphant progress.

After discussing the World Cup I began to ask the Prince about his latest literary achievements. (He has already written a most delightful and comprehensive book about the palaces of India.) I thought in answer to my question that he said he was in the middle of writing a book about Indian ports. I asked him what vintages he recommended but he informed me that the subject was forts and not ports.

We eventually got some more cricket at 2.45 p.m. on the Saturday afternoon. By then a draw was inevitable, and although this took some of the edge out of the play Athey's approaching hundred lent it a certain anticipation. He obliged after a slightly anxious period in the 90s. Ian Botham played one massive square cut before getting into a muddle against a lifter from Wasim Akram, but Bruce French batted well for the second Test match in succession. He has realised that if he is to stay in the England side he must turn himself into an all-rounder and this was further evidence of how hard he had worked at his batting since returning from Australia, England's tail-enders also made worthwhile contributions but when Graham Dilley was last out caught behind off Imran, the rain was already falling and it proved to be the last ball of the match.

After a blank day and a half it was a relief to have some cricket to talk about, but with two more blank days to come we had to exercise our imaginations to keep the programme going. It always surprises me how many people say they think we are at our best when there is no play. Maybe that is just their way of saying how bad we are when there is cricket. As it was, the chatter went on as chocolate cakes arrived and the occasional cork popped encouragingly.

While the Prince was our most memorable visitor, I had a lot of fun when Tom Graveney joined Ollie Milburn and myself for one 40-minute period. In this time we talked our way through Colin Cowdrey's tour of the West Indies in 1967–68. It was only the second tour I had covered and without any doubt whatever it was the most exciting Test series I have watched. England won 1–0 when Gary Sobers declared and left them to score 215 in 164 minutes on the last afternoon of the Fourth Test in Port-of-Spain. Thanks to marvellous batting by Cowdrey himself and Geoff Boycott, England won the day. England might have won the First Test, also at Port-of-Spain, but after tea on the last day could not find a way past the solid defence of Sobers and Wes Hall. England had all but won the Second Test in Kingston when Basil Butcher was caught behind off Basil D'Oliveira down the leg-side and the Sabina Park crowd rioted, which led to my first experience of tear-gas. After that Sobers made a brilliant hundred and on an unscheduled sixth day to compensate for the time lost to the rioters England came close to defeat. Tom himself was out when he pulled a ball against Steve Camacho at short-leg which rebounded to Charlie Griffith at mid-on.

The Third Test at Bridgetown was a dull draw. England won the Fourth and survived the last in Georgetown when, at the end of six days, England's last pair of Alan Knott and Jeff Jones played out the final balls of the match. It all made for a fascinating discussion as Tom, who played in all five Tests, and Ollie, who never quite got out of the Second XI, relived the tour both on and off the field.

All in all then, the Lord's Test may not have produced much cricket or a great deal of excitement, but if it brought *TMS* listeners half as much fun as it brought us in the box, they won't have had too bad a time of it.

ENGLAND 1ST INNINGS v PAKISTAN (2ND TEST) at LORD'S, LONDON, on 18, 19, 20, 21, 22 JUNE, 1987.

IN	OUT	MINS	No.	BATSMAN	HOW OUT	BOWLER	RUNS	WKT	TOTAL	6s	4s	BALLS	NOTES ON DISMISSAL TOSS: ENGLAND
11·00	2·28	170	1	B.C. BROAD	BOWLED	MUDASSAR	55	2	118	·	4	120	Through gate - played across line of inswinger.
11·00	11·45	45	2	R.T. ROBINSON	C⁺ SALIM YOUSUF	MOHSIN KAMAL	7	1	29	·	·	39	Edged leg-glance - departed reluctantly.
11·47	3·36	315	3	C.W.J. ATHEY	BOWLED	IMRAN	123	5	272	·	14	203	(1st in TESTS) Yorked middle stump - driving.
2·30	2·39	9	4	D.I. GOWER	C⁺ SALIM YOUSUF	MUDASSAR	8	3	128	·	2	9	Edged backfoot cover drive.
2·41	5·55	124	5	M.W. GATTING *	RUN OUT (MALIK/YOUSUF)		43	4	230	·	7	97	Failed to beat deep backward sq. leg's return.
5·57	4·11	90	6	B.N. FRENCH †	BOWLED	WASIM AKRAM	42	6	294	·	5	69	Played on - opened bat face too early.
3·38	4·45	48	7	I.T. BOTHAM	C⁺ MIANDAD	WASIM AKRAM	6	7	305	·	1	32	Gloved short ball gently to 2nd slip.
4·30	5·30	60	8	J.E. EMBUREY	RUN OUT (IJAZ/IMRAN)		12	9	340	·	2	37	Edmond's changed mind over run to mid-wicket.
4·47	5·12	25	9	N.A. FOSTER	BOWLED	ABDUL QADIR	21	8	329	·	4	22	Middle stump - missed vast heave at straight ball.
5·14	(6·01)	47	10	P.H. EDMONDS	NOT OUT		17			·	1	32	
5·32	6·01	29	11	G.R. DILLEY	C⁺ SALIM YOUSUF	IMRAN	17	10	368	·	3	24	Faint edge - beaten by pace.

* CAPTAIN † WICKET-KEEPER

EXTRAS	b - lb 12 w 1 nb 4	17

0s 43s 684 balls (inc. 7 no-balls)

TOTAL (112·5 OVERS - 489 MINUTES) **368** ALL OUT at 6·01 pm on 3rd day

13 OVERS 5 BALLS/HOUR
3·26 RUNS/OVER
53 RUNS/100 BALLS

UMPIRES:
D.J. CONSTANT & A.G.T. WHITEHEAD

BOWLER	O	M	R	W		HRS	OVERS	RUNS		RUNS	MINS	OVERS	LAST 50 (in mins)
IMRAN KHAN	34·5	7	90	2	√/	1	12	41		50	76	15·2	76
WASIM AKRAM	28	1	98	2	4/-	2	15	38		100	142	32·2	66
MOHSIN KAMAL	9	2	42	1	-	3	14	48		150	216	50·1	74
ABDUL QADIR	25	1	100	1	√-	4	15	35		200	284	67·0	68
MUDASSAR NAZAR	16	6	26	2	√-	5	14	59		250	350	81·3	66
			12	2		6	14	48		300	404	94·2	54
						7	13	39		350	465	107·5	61
	112·5	17	368	10		8	13	54					

2ND NEW BALL taken at 3·35pm 3rd day
- ENGLAND 271·4 after 85 overs

LUNCH: 80 - 1 (28 OVERS / 122 MIN) BROAD 29*(46) ATHEY 35*(75)
TEA: 164 - 3 (57 OVERS / 242 MIN) ATHEY 70*(124) GATTING 16*(19)
STUMPS: 231-4 (1st DAY) (73 OVERS / 313 MIN) ATHEY 107*(166) FRENCH 1*(4)
NO PLAY 2nd DAY. 3rd DAY - START DELAYED UNTIL 2·45pm
TEA: 294-6 (92·5 OVERS / 309 MIN) BOTHAM 5*(25)

WKT	PARTNERSHIP		RUNS	MINS
1st	Broad	Robinson	29	45
2nd	Broad	Athey	89	123
3rd	Athey	Gower	10	9
4th	Athey	Gatting	102	124
5th	Athey	French	42	49
6th	French	Botham	22	33
7th	Botham	Emburey	11	15
8th	Emburey	Foster	24	25
9th	Emburey	Edmonds	11	16
10th	Edmonds	Dilley	28	29

368

COMPILED by BILL FRINDALL

PAKISTAN 1ST INNINGS   IN REPLY TO ENGLAND'S 368 ALL OUT

IN	OUT	MINS	No.	BATSMAN	HOW OUT	BOWLER	RUNS	WKT	TOTAL	6s	4s	BALLS	NOTES ON DISMISSAL
			1	MUDASSAR NAZAR									
			2	SHOAIB MOHD									
			3	MANSOOR AKHTAR									
			4	JAVED MIANDAD									
			5	SALIM MALIK									
			6	IJAZ AHMED	DID NOT BAT								
			7	IMRAN KHAN *									
			8	SALIM YOUSUF †									
			9	WASIM AKRAM									
			10	ABDUL QADIR									
			11	MOHSIN KAMAL									

* CAPTAIN † WICKET-KEEPER

EXTRAS	b lb w nb	

TOTAL ____

OVERS
BALLS/HOUR
RUNS/OVER
RUNS/100 BALLS

BOWLER	O	M	R	W		HRS	OVERS	RUNS		RUNS	MINS	OVERS	LAST 50 (in mins)

RAIN PREVENTED START OF PAKISTAN'S INNINGS (NO PLAY ON FOURTH OR FIFTH DAYS).

MATCH DRAWN

MATCH AWARD: C.W.J. ATHEY
(Adjudicator: T.E. BAILEY)

WKT	PARTNERSHIP		RUNS	MINS

COMPILED BY BILL FRINDALL

An Off-the-Field Hat-Trick

Brian Johnston

Most of us will always remember 1987 as the Madam Butterfly summer – One Fine Day! But I shall also recall a hat-trick of unusual and unlikely events off the field. I danced to rock and roll in the Royal Tennis Court at Lord's, saw a total of 733 on the Grandstand scoreboard, and danced the Lambeth Walk in the dignified and sacrosanct Council Chamber at Broadcasting House.

I'll take them in order. The night of 26 March was one of the stormiest nights St John's Wood has ever known. Goodness knows at how many miles per hour the winds blew. When I looked out of the window in the morning our garden was strewn with debris from the surrounding trees. This day, 27 March, was chosen by the MCC Bicentenary Committee for the Spring Ball, one of several celebrations leading up to the climax of the Bicentenary Match at Lord's, MCC v The Rest of the World. Other events were to be a dinner in the Long Room, a lunch in Dorset Square and a dinner in the Guildhall.

For the Ball a giant marquee had been erected on the Nursery ground, large enough for 1,000 people to dine and dance. At 10.00 a.m. the whole thing collapsed, following an enormous rent in the roofing. Underneath the mass of canvas were the tables and chairs, the sprung parquet dance floor, the glasses, plates and cutlery and all the electrical equipment set up for the bands and the cabaret. Surely one of the greatest disasters ever suffered by the Premier Club.

But there were no panic stations: just instant action. With two Colonels and a Wing-Commander on the secretariat an immediate 'council of war' was convened under the chairmanship of Hubert Doggart. There would be no surrender. The simple solution – just transfer the whole Ball to the inside of the pavilion and its precincts. The whole of the Lord's staff volunteered to help; secretariat, groundstaff, gatemen, security officers and the catering staff. Just imagine trying to move all that paraphernalia across the ground, and then to arrange the tables and chairs and the food and the drink into the limited space available. But to the eternal credit of the MCC staff the miracle was achieved. A few of the guests had heard about the disaster and did not turn up. But about 800 of the original 1,000 arrived, some unsuspecting, others, having heard news of the disaster, not knowing what to expect. On arrival every guest was handed the following information:

We regret that the Marquee in which the Ball was to have been held blew down this morning. However MCC are not prepared to let a minor problem such as this spoil the evening, and the following arrangements have therefore been made:

Entrance: By either door of the Pavilion with cloakrooms at the top of the stairs.

Champagne Reception followed by Buffet Supper served in the Long Room and writing room. (Thanks to the great efforts of Searcys the Menu will be virtually the same as before.) Eating and Sitting-Out areas will be:

The Long Room

The Writing Room

The Committee Dining Room (top floor)

The Members Bar (top floor)

Dancing to Joe Loss and his band and Tropic Isles in the Royal Tennis Court. The Memorial Gallery will be open until midnight. In spite of everything we hope you will still have a wonderful evening.

And we did! Maybe it was a bit of a crush; true, we had to collect our food instead of being waited on; and the cabaret by Elaine Paige had to be cancelled because of lack of space and damage to the sound equipment. But everyone seemed determined to support the great efforts of the MCC staff and tremendous fun was had by all. Joe Loss, aged 77, was terrific and played every kind of music right through to the early hours from old-fashioned waltzes to rock and roll. The dance floor had been relaid in the Tennis Court, which made a most unusual but magnificent ballroom. So that's how I came to dance in the Tennis Court and I wouldn't have missed it for the world. Oh, and by the way, there was an extra bonus for the ladies – they were able to beard the sanctity of those exclusive male preserves – the two dressing-rooms, whether officially or not, I'm not sure. But there were drinks and suppers being consumed where all the great players have changed and put on their pads and boxes, quite something to boast about at the next Women's Institute Meeting!

On 20 May I was back at Lord's to record my final *Down Your Way*. I had taken over from Franklin Englemann ('Jingle') in March 1972, when he died suddenly just after recording his 733rd programme. By 1987 I had been presenting the programme for 15 years and realised that by May I would have reached the same total as Jingle. So I thought I would copy the generous gesture of John Francome in 1982. He was lying second to Peter Scudamore in the National Hunt Jockeys' Table when Peter had a bad fall which prevented him from riding for the rest of the season. John Francome went on riding until in the middle of one afternoon he drew level with Peter's number of winners. There and then he lay down his saddle and his whip and refused to ride any more that season.

So I asked the BBC to release me when I reached 733 and was allowed to choose my final venue. And, of course, it had to be Lord's, who very kindly gave me permission to invade them and carry out my usual six interviews. I say 'invade' because the national press, televison and radio had become surprisingly interested in covering this final fling of mine, and there must have been 30 to 40 cameramen and news correspondents to cover the event.

Colonel John Stephenson knew *some* people would be coming but got the shock of his life when he saw this large gang of mediamen all standing out on his beloved square. But Lord's went to great trouble to make us all welcome and to make my last day a happy one. On arrival at the ground I spotted that the total on the Grandstand scoreboard read 733. This was the largest score it had ever recorded, the previous highest being 729 in the 1930 Test by Australia. On that occasion the scoreboard could not cope – they never expected anything higher than 600. So they had to hang out a seven over the six in the frame. They obviously learnt their lesson after that, because my 733 clicked up like any other score.

As usual we had six interviews in our 45-minute programme and here they are in their final batting order, together with the piece of music each guest chose:

1 Colin Cowdrey, president of MCC, 'Underneath the Arches' sung by Flanagan and Allen.
2 Stephen Green, curator, 'Bredon Hill' sung by Gervase Elwes (tenor).
3 Lt-Col John Stephenson, secretary of MCC, 'Jerusalem' sung by Massed English Male Chorus and played by The Royal Doulton Band.
4 Mick Hunt, head groundsman, 'Our House' sung by Bing Crosby.
5 Nancy Doyle, manager, Committee Dining-Room, 'Bad Habits' sung by Billy Field.
6 Denis Compton, Middlesex and England, 'My Way' sung by Frank Sinatra.

From my selection of people I did my best to cover all aspects of Lord's and to suit their movements we recorded them in a different sequence to the final batting order. We began recording in the morning, my last interview before lunch being Denis Compton. Colin Cowdrey had organised a lunch party up in the Committee Dining-Room, prepared by Nancy, who has a worldwide reputation among cricketers for keeping the best table anywhere on the cricket circuit. We lunched well – possibly too well! My first victim after lunch was Colin himself, and for the first time in all the previous 732 *Down Your Ways*, I forgot to ask him *before* the interview what music he was going to choose. At the end of our conversation I asked him what he would like us to play. To my dismay he said, '"My Way" please, sung by Frank Sinatra'. Exactly what Denis had chosen just before lunch. So we had to stop the recording and ask him to choose something else. Strangely without any hesitation he chose my signature tune: 'Underneath the Arches' sung by Bud Flanagan and Chesney Allen. It was strange because, unknown to him, it's the only tune I can play all the way through on the piano, and in my *In Town Tonight* days I had sung it outside the stage door of the Victoria Palace with Bud Flanagan himself.

There was a bit of a lump in my throat when Sinatra sang 'My Way' but I had had a good innings of 733 scored in 13,400 hours and at my age one has to stop *something* at some point.

And so to the third part of my hat-trick – dancing the Lambeth Walk in the Council Chamber at Broadcasting House. The Chamber is a crescent-shaped room on the first floor at the front of the building, overlooking Oxford Circus. It has an austere atmosphere about it as befits a room used for important meetings, conferences and the odd farewell cocktail party or dinner. Pat Ewing, Head of Radio Sport and

BJ with his final guest for Down Your Way –
Denis Compton. Pauline Johnston

At the door of the Long Room, B.J. waits for
MCC President Colin Cowdrey's choice of
record. Pauline Johnston

Outside Broadcasts, very kindly decided that she and the department would give me a 75th birthday party. It was scheduled for 26 June, two days after my birthday, and she asked me to choose the guests from all the colleagues and friends with whom I had worked at the BBC. The final count was about 50, with one or two like Paul Fox, Frank Bough, Peter Dimmock, Robert Hudson and Don Mosey sadly being unable to come. But all my BBC activities were well represented. *Test Match Special*, *Down Your Way*, Royal occasions, *In Town Tonight* the Boat Race etc. Pat was determined that it would not be just another dinner, and decided to add a marvellous ingredient – a 1920s jazz band. Music in the Council Chamber and jazz at that! It was not easy for her to get permission for this break from tradition in the Holy of Holies. I believe she started at the bottom and had to work her way right up to the Director-General before she could get permission. It was a complete surprise to me when the high, imposing doors were flung open as we had just sat down to dine. Through the doors marched Humphrey Carpenter and his Vile Bodies playing 'the Knightsbridge March' – signature tune of *In Town Tonight*. And what a rendering! The Chamber echoed to the sound of trumpets, trombones and double bass. They proceeded to play throughout dinner all my favourite tunes of the 1920s and 1930s. At this stage they were not too loud, so we could all hear each other chattering away like mad. And when you get a 'chatter of commentators' all together you have to be pretty quick to get a word in edgeways. Pat made a kind and felicitous speech and then presented me with a giant cake, bedecked as a cricket match with fielders, batsmen, stumps and all. This was followed by a beautiful decanter of Caithness glass with a charming and flattering message on the front. On the back were engravings depicting my BBC activities: a rowing eight for the Boat Race; violets for *In Town Tonight* (remember those old flowersellers' voices as they sat at the base of Eros – 'Violets, lovely violets . . . '); a disc for *Down Your Way*, the dome of St Paul's for Royal occasions – and a batsman driving a ball. It was a truly magnificent present and is standing proudly on my mantelpiece as I write. It's something which I shall always treasure. I did my best to say thank you to everyone and then the band really struck up. Everyone began to sing and dance and it was then that the Lambeth Walk was danced in and out of the tables. I shall never forget Rex Alston – a young 86 with his stick held high in the air, forgetting painful hips and knees and leading the dance like a two-year-old. And Jim Swanton – only six years younger – made a very good job of it, too. Lupino Lane, the originator, would have been proud of us all. There was also, thoughtfully, a piano provided and we all gathered round to sing with the best 'pub pianist' in the business, Alun Williams at the keys. It really was a super evening which, even at an age when one's memory begins to fail, I shall *never* forget.

Cliff Morgan told me some time later that the noise from the band spread all over Broadcasting House. So much so that down in the main marble hall all the commissionaires and cleaners were doing a conga round the hall and along the corridors. What would Lord Reith have thought of it all? I couldn't help thinking of this when we were dancing in the Council Chamber where portraits of past director-generals are hung all round the room. Lord Reith is looking fiercely down with his beetling black eyebrows outdoing even those of Denis Healey. Reith was a puritan, a strict disciplinarian and always set and expected the highest standard of behaviour from the BBC staff.

One evening in the 1930s he was touring the building and looked in at one of the drama studios. To his horror he saw one of the drama producers making love to one of the actresses on the studio table. He rushed back to his office and summoned one of his assistants. 'I've just seen so-and-so making love to so-and-so on the studio table. Get rid of them both at once, and tell them never to darken the doors of Broadcasting House again.' 'But Sir,' stammered his assistant, 'you can't do that. He's our best producer and she is the outstanding actress in the Rep.' 'I'm sorry', said Reith, 'I've made up my mind. Do as I say. Get rid of them both'. 'But Sir,' said the assistant, trying another tack, 'the play which they are rehearsing has been advertised in *Radio Times*. We would have to cancel it and that would cause an even bigger scandal.' Reith thought for a moment or two then made up his mind. 'Very well. There may be something in what you say. Then get rid of the table!'

But let's hope that from his vantage point on the wall he enjoyed this unique evening as much as we all did.

The Third Test at Headingley

Don Mosey

To put into perspective England's only defeat in the series – but a vitally important one since it cost them the rubber for the first time against Pakistan in this country – it is necessary to consider at some length the condition of the pitch.

Headingley is renowned for one particular phenomenon: when the sun shines the ball, by and large, does not move much in the air but when cloud comes over it starts, otherwise unaccountably, to swing. Those of us who know the ground well have debated this matter with learned and scientific minds for many years. We have had treatises posted to us from such institutions as Cambridge University arguing cogently and forcefully that it is aerodynamically impossible for a leather-encased spheroid projected by the human arm to move in the air *in any circumstances*. We have taken delivery of manuscripts running to 20 pages and covered in equations which would have caused problems for Einstein which prove conclusively that the ball *cannot* swing. Proving it, that is, to the scientist.

To each of these protestations, our resident expert in these matters, Frederick Seward Trueman, replies quite simply: 'Let him go out there with a bat in his hands and I'll *show* him that it'll swing'. And there is no doubt – even at the age of 56, Fred, by a combination of body-movement, arm-position, moment-of-release, fingers across the seam and shine on one side of the ball *would* be able to swing the ball in the air if atmospheric conditions were right.

That is one thing. It would require, in addition to cloudy conditions giving a slightly heavier atmosphere than bright sunlight produces, a great deal of technical expertise or an equal amount of God-given natural talent. If the bowler possesses either there is nothing anyone can do about it. It is then up to the batsman to exercise all his powers to counter this form of attack by judging which ball to play, which to leave alone. All this has nothing whatever to do with the state of the pitch.

Seam bowling is something else altogether and it has a *great deal* to do with the state of the pitch. 'Leaving a lot of grass on the pitch' is a metaphorical way of saying that the groundsman has not cropped the playing part of the ground right down to the roots. Even a modest growth will cause the ball to move laterally to some extent if the ball pitches with its seam angled either way because the seam, slightly raised from the smoother outer surface of the ball, can 'bite' on the sort of resistant pitch which is provided by a fraction of an inch of grass.

All right so far? And to those of you who are already asking 'Why is he telling us all this? It's elementary to anyone who has played any sort of different cricket', let me say at once that obviously not everyone *does* understand it. Before the Headingley Test one highly-respected national newspaper offered the view that 'the seamer's wicket would help David Capel's outswing', which is the most arrant nonsense from a quarter where one expects better things. And another newspaper – not one of the rubbishy tabloids – offered an identical view of Capel's bowling, but in the context of a pitch at Northampton on which Yorkshire had just been summarily dismissed. Even in the court of king television this sort of mistake can be made. Watching the Leicestershire v Northants game in the NatWest Trophy I heard one of the experts – though not, mercifully, a regular – apply the description 'outswinger' to a delivery which patently obviously did not swing at all, but which moved away off the seam.

So all this has to be borne in mind when considering the various criticisms which were levelled at the Headingley wicket – after England had been bowled out cheaply and subsequently lost. The pitch there has been criticised on a number of occasions in recent years. It has been 'knocked' for helping spin bowlers as well as seamers. Quite simply, it has become fashionable for one side or the other to blame the wicket after being defeated on it because they know they will get support from sections of the media. The perfect Test pitch (as described by the idealists) is one which starts 'with a bit of pace in it', encouraging the quicker bowlers to put everything they have got into their work and the batsmen to play strokes because the ball is coming on to the bat, which then begins to assist the spinners as it becomes a little worn and/or dusty later in the game. The school of thought which decrees this appears to believe that a good Test match is only possible if a huge number of runs is scored and I have to ask, 'Why?' A Test is a contest of cricket skills at their highest levels *and in all their forms*. Why must bowling be reduced to cannon fodder to make it a Roman holiday for batsmen before we can have a 'good' Test? By definition it should be as near as possible to an even contest.

So if Old Trafford, Edgbaston and The Oval are going to cosset and featherbed the batsmen, what is wrong with at least one wicket in the series which gives some help to the bowler? Do we not then get a serious test of batting techniques and stroke-making ability? There is no doubt an argument for those primarily concerned with finance, those who view with apprehension an empty or near-empty ground for an hour or two on the final day. But would those fears arise if modern batsmen had the technique to compete with good bowling in relatively helpful conditions? Would not better technique enable batsmen to resist while slowing down the scoring for some less gifted players, thus prolonging the match to the satisfaction of those who cry out for income, but at the same time providing the fascination of a duel between competitive skills for the discerning spectator?

Headingley has been helpful to a certain extent to bowlers for some years and was more particularly so in the early part of the 1987 season. There is no more conscientious groundsman anywhere in the world than Keith Boyce. If he ever has time to sleep he can dream only about his beloved turf, of which he has an encyclopaedic knowledge. But he has been beset by problems not of his making, only one of which was the wretched weather of the summer of 1987. It is not that he did not understand the problems. I have talked to him before Benson & Hedges games and before County Championship matches. He has said, realistically – perhaps fatalistically – that 'it's a 180 wicket' or 'a 250 wicket'. And invariably he has been correct to within a run or two. That suggests *deep* knowledge.

The Test pitch at Headingley fell into the '250, perhaps 300' category, and it was not Keith Boyce's fault that England were bowled out for 136 on it after winning the toss. To say that Gatting was wrong to elect to bat is to say that Foster and Dilley would have bowled as well as Imran Khan, who destroyed England's early batting and with it their later confidence, before the clocks had struck 12 noon on the first morning. In fact Foster (who got the figures) and Dilley (who suffered agonies of misfortune) *did* bowl well throughout the Pakistan innings, but neither has the extreme pace of Imran which was what accounted for the early collapse. And, quite simply, Pakistan batted better than England. Broad, whose defence against genuinely quick bowling is generally admirable, was surprised by the extra bounce extracted by Imran while at the same time moving the ball away from the left-hander; Robinson, as has been suspected for some time, has no real technical answer to extra pace and succumbed to it without delay; and Athey, despite his understandable and understood move to Gloucestershire, occupies a place in native Yorkshire hearts, which were saddened to see a departure hastened by poor application of basics. Gower, not for the first time, indicated a certain laziness of evasive action (for which all his grace and elegance shout in denial, only for fallibility to rear its ugly head when least expected) and played on; and Gatting, who by this time ought to have known better, took no action at all to avoid the lbw.

By 11.58 a.m. on the first morning of his first Test match, Northamptonshire's David Capel (picked primarily to cover Botham's suspect bowling as third seamer – how many all-rounders in history have enjoyed that luxury?) found himself at the crease with an heroic batting performance required of him. He duly supplied that, partnering Botham in a mid-innings stand of 54, and gathered strength from the tail to be eighth out at 133. The total progressed no further with Edmonds failing to trouble the scorers beyond the recording of two deliveries, the second of which accounted for him, to give that most enthusiastic of appealers, Salim Yousuf, his fourth catch behind the stumps.

By close of play on the first day, Pakistan had reached 76 for two wickets, Mudassar uncharacteristically playing across the line to be lbw and Shoaib unable to cope with unexpected bounce to be caught behind. By lunch on the second day, Pakistan had equalled England's total with six wickets in hand but England had received a bonus of incalculable worth – the wicket of the immensely gifted Javed Miandad for nought. Foster moved the ball away from him with perfect line and length and Javed was well caught by Gatting at second slip.

After lunch, Salim Yousuf (who had been posted as nightwatchman the previous evening) went serenely on, enjoying himself hugely until he fell to a second-slip catch, this time by Athey. Foster having disposed of Mansoor Akhtar in the early part of the morning, had taken the first five wickets to fall. Salim Malik now settled into a partnership of 56 with Imran (who became the sixth successive victim of Foster at 208 for 6) and another of 72 with Ijaz Ahmed. This was the first view for many of us of the 18-year-old batsman who looks to be one of the best prospects worldwide, and he played some delightful strokes in his 50. Salim Malik, in the meantime, had broken the Foster sequence of wicket-taking by mistiming a drive off Edmonds' bowling and giving a catch to Gower at short extra-cover. He was on 99 and perhaps contributed to his own downfall by spending an introspective 62 minutes in the 90s but it is difficult not to feel sympathy with any batsman, friend or foe, who falls on that mark. At 280 for 7, a lead of 144, Pakistan slept easy that night and Saturday morning brought a less conventional but highly entertaining change of tempo as Wasim Akram, (who joins Lancashire in 1988) smote the ball lustily to all quarters.

He finally left to a most distinguished catch by Edmonds who, morosely loitering at deep third man with no one, for a change, to talk to save the spectators, saw a huge slice by Wasim curl in a tantalising arc towards him. Edmonds lumbered in like the good rugby No 8 forward he once was, corner-flagging, and then launched himself forward to hold the catch and hang on to it as he sprawled full-length. Abdul Qadir provided modest compensation for the perspiring Dilley and it was Mohsin Kamal who got the little star beside his name as the not out batsman.

Foster's career-best eight for 107 was just reward for intelligent use of a pitch which helped him to move the ball away off the seam, bowling up the hill from the football end. Dilley, who toiled mightily and bowled more than the occasional beautiful outswinger, could induce no one to get a touch. Though it would have detracted from Foster's performance in terms of figures, Dilley's bowling deserved a better reward. Capel, alas, having performed nobly with the bat was ineffectual with the ball in conditions which should have suited him well. Edmonds, as so often happens, found himself unable to harness wicket-taking to the imagination and inventiveness of his bowling. Pakistan, all out with 353 fractionally after noon on the third day, contemplated a lead of 217 and something more than eight periods of play to dispose of England again, if the weather held good.

The sun had blazed down for the whole of the match up to this point and there was no immediate forecast of a change. Nevertheless, Imran Khan – not without experience of sudden changes in Britain's climate – was taking no chances. By lunch both openers were back in the pavilion, Broad in rather controversial circumstances. As he tried to move bat and gloves out of the firing line of a ball lifting outside the off-stump, the usual impassioned appeal from Salim Yousuf rent the air. Broad immediately tried to indicate that the ball had brushed a glove which had been withdrawn from the bat-handle and was aggrieved to find the umpire's finger going up. If the hand had been removed when the ball touched the glove the correct decision was, of course, not out, but it was a desperately close thing for an umpire to have to work out, given the pace at which Imran was bowling and the flurry of bat and gloves which followed. With the benefit of hindsight and the slow-motion play-back on television it becomes, of course, a different matter altogether and it is possible to make out a case for an injustice having been done. But umpires don't have a slow-motion play-back which, in itself, can on occasions be misleading. They have to call it as they see it, and all that can have been seen there was a blur.

It was a chronically difficult decision to have to make and if a mistake occurred it would be a very hard man indeed who blamed the umpire. Broad had received just a couple of balls and obviously there has to be sympathy for him. Robinson received four before edging a catch to second slip and Athey and Gower averted further disaster until lunch (44–2). Less than half-an-hour afterwards Imran struck two more vital blows, Athey getting one which kept a trifle low to find him in front of the stumps and Gatting giving a catch to second slip. Gower soldiered on to finish top scorer with 55 before once again playing on and another rescue act by Capel was called for. Before the close of another disastrous day, Richards had provided Imran with his 300th Test wicket and Botham (batting at number eight and with a runner because of an injured foot) fell to a cracking catch at point by Mudassar. At stumps, England were 186 for 7 and with Botham gone there was little hope of a 1981-style miracle. Just 24 minutes were required on the Monday for Wasim and Imran to mop up the last three wickets, Capel going for 28 very brave runs, Foster for 22 and Dilley for no score. Imran's 7 for 40 return gave a match return of 10 for 77 and won him the Man of the Match award. There could have been no other choice; he had given us a brilliant display of high-quality fast bowling in reasonably helpful conditions and England's batsmen had no answer to it.

But against bowling which was currently as good as England could muster, Pakistan had shown how to bat on a seamer's pitch. It used to be said, with patronising mock-sympathy, that teams coming here from the sub-continent were at a serious disadvantage when our wickets helped seam bowling. Here a team had showed an England XI how to do it. Somehow it seems to have been overlooked that many of the Pakistanis, quite apart from Imran and Javed in the County Championship, have spent a good deal of time here in league cricket and are no strangers at

for the replays. I can reveal that few press box TV monitors are tuned into the cricket.

I was a little surprised when my host introduced me as the editor of *Foreplay Annual*. I hope he was referring to *Playfair Cricket Annual*, but they do say that all publicity is good publicity. It did appear to intrigue a number of the ladies, who seemed particularly interested in my views on Botham.

Broad and Robinson added a careful 54 runs in 27 overs before lunch. I found it absorbing but my fleet-dealing companions were eager for more excitement. So were most of the spectators I met during my book-signing stint beside the main gate. Many dozed off during the afternoon as the Notts pair took their opening stand to 119 before Imran's out-swinger found the edge of the left-handed Broad's attempted off-drive.

My first deadline was 4.15 p.m. and I was very grateful for that dismissal. Athey eventually contributed to the action-packed drama by totally misjudging a straight ball which Imran bowled wide of the crease, after 27 runless minutes. At tea England were 155-2 with Robinson's unbeaten 80 dominating my piece.

Gower provided some classic strokes which included ten boundaries in a richly entertaining innings of 61. Then, at 5.51 p.m., came the day's most dramatic phase. Armed with the second new ball, Imran found new energy and inspiration. His third over gained the wickets of Gower and nightwatchman French (a negative choice with 6.4 overs of the day left). Enter SuperBoth. Eschewing helmet, he took on the bouncers and blistering pace of the warrior Khan. It was exhilarating stuff. The Peugeot fleet men were enthralled. I rewrote my report.

Copy filed, I joined the players for a quick glass of falling-over water at Cornhill's daily end-of-play reception. It is always a delight to dissect the day's play with some of the protagonists and to meet the sponsors' guests, many of them retired Test players. There was no scarcity of hospitality during this Test; it was all too easy to become as sponsored as a newt. Nor was there a shortage of invitations to evening thrashes. We had already enjoyed an open-air feast in the grounds of the Health Clinic run by former England physiotherapist Bernard Thomas, and a superb Pakistani meal at Mushtaq Mohammad's house. Monday was to witness a memorable party hosted by Frances and Phil Edmonds to launch 'Felini', their spectacular designer store in the centre of Birmingham.

Sunday provided a welcome respite from the pressures of a Test match. Mercifully the brief experiment of playing five-day matches without a rest day proved unpopular with English spectators. I spent a pleasant busman's holiday playing cricket for the Lord's Taverners at Stratford. The tree-fringed ground is set beside the Avon opposite the famous theatre and will soon boast a palatial pavilion. Stratford Cricket Club's excessive hospitality has ensured that this is one of the few Taverners' fixtures to be played every season.

When the Test resumed on Monday, Gatting completed his eighth hundred in 27 Tests (having waited 30 matches for his first). With Emburey, his vice-captain, in faithful support, he added 143 for the seventh wicket. England's total of 521 gave

Botham at Edgbaston. His hook to long leg virtually ended England's chance of a remarkable victory.
All-Sport/Adrian Murrell

Inset: *The Sheriff of Edgbaston – the Mushtaq Kid.*　　　Peter Baxter

them a lead of 82 and was gleaned from 22 fewer balls than Pakistan's 439. Few punters would have bet on a result when England's first innings ended at 5.03 p.m. on the fourth day.

The tedium of an apparently inevitable draw was relieved by the arrival of Mushtaq Mohammad, dressed as a cowboy. Usually undemonstrative, he favours sober suits and jackets. But there he was with the full outfit, down to spurs and six-shooter. It was a little off-putting to hear the expert comments in a Pakistani accent emerging from beneath a stetson. Grossly upstaged, poor Johnners was most put out. Mushtaq's Club, Old Hill CC, were responsible for this bizarre behaviour. It was a forfeit imposed on him for imparting wrong information on air about the team's progress in the Village Knockout Cup. When Old Hill won the final at Lord's a few weeks later I was enticed into their dressing-room and made to wear the horse's head which completed the outfit. In 1977 I spent a Test match Saturday at The Oval disguised as an Arab. Trends in cricket have always been set slowly.

Mushy arrived in mufti on the final morning and had been presented with a curry cake by some of his friends. BJ greedily seized a chunk, smelt it and asked for a window to be opened.

By lunch Pakistan had reached 79-1. They were still three runs in arrears, and we were recommending the introduction of a euthanasia clause to terminate such painful contests. But, mysteriously refreshed by the interval, Foster and Botham had other ideas and within an hour the tourists were effectively 34-6. The unbelievable had happened: the tourists had relaxed and suddenly England had conjured a winning position from nowhere. Only an obdurate rearguard action led by Imran, on the ground where he made his Test debut in 1971 at the age of 18, prolonged the struggle into its ultimate phase.

England's target was 124 runs from 18 overs, an asking rate of 6.9 runs per over. Some brilliantly improvised strokes by Broad ensured that they were exactly on course at the half-way mark with just three wickets down. But Imran kept his troops on a close rein. Their excellent fielding seized three run-outs and some poor cricket by England enabled Pakistan to preserve their lead.

Adjudicator Robin Jackman's decision to give the match award to Gatting and not Imran will be debated whenever the match is discussed. Cricket being a team game I have never been in favour of this particular sponsors' gimmick. My own choice would have favoured Imran for taking eight wickets on a bland pitch, batting for over two hours to ensure the final equation and, above all, maintaining calm and control during England's dramatic thrust for victory.

PAKISTAN 1st INNINGS v. ENGLAND (4th TEST) at EDGBASTON, BIRMINGHAM on 23, 24, 25, 27, 28 JULY, 1987   TOSS: ENGLAND

IN	OUT	MINS	No.	BATSMAN	HOW OUT	BOWLER	RUNS	WKT	TOTAL	6s	4s	BALLS	NOTES ON DISMISSAL
11.00	2.21	417	1	MUDASSAR NAZAR	LBW	DILLEY	124	4	284	·	16	361	9th [1st overs, 3rd at wide mne] Missed slight breakback in poor light.
11.00	12.05	65	2	SHOAIB MOHD.	c FOSTER	EDMONDS	18	1	44	·	2	49	Lofted drive - held at 2nd attempt by mid-off running back.
12.07	2.14	86	3	MANSOOR AKHTAR	BOWLED	FOSTER	26	2	83	·	4	87	Played on - inside edge to 'walking' drive.
2.16	5.08	151	4	JAVED MIANDAD	LBW	DILLEY	75	3	218	1	8	145	Played across near-yorker.
5.10	3.00	130	5	SALIM MALIK	c FRENCH	DILLEY	24	5	289	·	3	95	Edged low to keeper - right-handed catch diving in front of 1st slip
2.23	3.30	49	6	IJAZ AHMED	LBW	BOTHAM	20	7	317	·	4	35	Missed inswinger.
3.01	-	1	7	IMRAN KHAN *	c EMBUREY	DILLEY	0	6	289	·	·	·	Edged outswinger to 1st slip (1st ball)
3.04	(6.26)	182	8	SALIM YOUSUF †	NOT OUT		91	·	·	·	14	151	HS in TESTS
3.32	4.44	52	9	WASIM AKRAM	c BOTHAM	FOSTER	26	8	360	1	4	44	Edged waist-high to 2nd slip. FOSTER's 50th TEST WICKET
4.46	5.22	27	10	ABDUL QADIR	c EDMONDS	DILLEY	6	9	384	·	·	30	Fended short ball low to gully's left - 2-handed full-length catch.
5.24	6.26	62	11	MOHSIN KAMAL	RUN OUT [DILLEY]		10	10	439	·	·	47	Backed up for run to short 3rd man - sent back.

* CAPTAIN † WICKET-KEEPER

EXTRAS b 4 lb 11 w 1 nb 3   19

2s 56s 1045 balls (inc 4 nb)

TOTAL (173.3 OVERS - 623 MINUTES) 439

UMPIRES: B.J. MEYER & A.G.T. WHITEHEAD

16 OVERS 4 BALLS/HOUR
2.53 RUNS/OVER
42 RUNS/100 BALLS

BOWLER	O	M	R	W	%	HRS	OVERS	RUNS
DILLEY	35	6	92	5	4	1	17	41
FOSTER	37	8	107	2	·	2	21	29
EMBUREY	26	7	48	0	·	3	17	31
EDMONDS	24.3	12	50	1	4	4	18	52
BOTHAM	48	13	121	1	·	5	17	54
GATTING	3	0	6	0	·	6	15	43
		15	1			7	15	34
	173.3	46	439	9		8	15	39
						9	15	43
						10	15	59

2nd NEW BALL taken at 4.45pm
- PAKISTAN 198-2 after 86.2 overs

RUNS	MINS	OVERS	LAST 50 (in mins)
50	78	22.5	48
100	178	54.3	100
150	238	71.5	60
200	286	87.1	48
250	360	104.5	74
300	451	128.0	92
350	508	142.1	57
400	572	157.4	64

LUNCH: 70-1 [38 OVERS / 120 MIN] MUDASSAR 32* (120) AKHTAR 15* (58)

TEA: 153-2 [73 OVERS / 240 MIN] MUDASSAR 64* (240) MIANDAD 35* (85)

STUMPS: 250-3 [105 OVERS / 361 MIN] MUDASSAR 102* (361) MALIK 13* (52)
(1st DAY)

2nd DAY : START DELAYED UNTIL 1.25pm - 26 OVERS LOST

TEA: 346-7 [142 OVERS / 507 MIN] YOUSUF 20* (66) AKRAM 21* (38)

WKT	PARTNERSHIP		RUNS	MINS
1st	Mudassar	Shoaib	44	65
2nd	Mudassar	Akhtar	39	86
3rd	Mudassar	Miandad	135	151
4th	Mudassar	Malik	66	109
5th	Malik	Ijaz	5	19
6th	Ijaz	Imran	0	1
7th	Ijaz	Yousuf	28	26
8th	Yousuf	Akram	43	52
9th	Yousuf	Qadir	24	27
10th	Yousuf	Kamal	55	62
			439	

COMPILED by BILL FRINDALL

ENGLAND 1st INNINGS   IN REPLY TO PAKISTAN'S 439 ALL OUT

IN	OUT	MINS	No.	BATSMAN	HOW OUT	BOWLER	RUNS	WKT	TOTAL	6s	4s	BALLS	NOTES ON DISMISSAL
6.36	2.41	208	1	B.C. BROAD	c SALIM YOUSUF	IMRAN	54	1	119	·	5	148	Edged drive at outswinger.
6.36	4.05	272	2	R.T. ROBINSON	c SALIM YOUSUF	AKRAM	80	3	157	·	11	207	Edged drive at near-wide.
2.42	3.09	27	3	C.W.J. ATHEY	BOWLED	IMRAN	0	2	132	·	·	17	Bowled through gate - misjudged line - bowled wide of crease.
3.11	5.51	139	4	D.I. GOWER	c SALIM YOUSUF	IMRAN	61	4	251	·	10	105	Edged push drive at ball slanted across him.
4.06	4.25	401	5	M.W. GATTING *	c AKRAM	IMRAN	124	8	484	1	16	281	8th in TESTS Mid-on - simple catch - mistimed drive.
5.52	5.54	2	6	B.N. FRENCH †	BOWLED	IMRAN	0	5	251	·	·	2	Late on brutal breakback - stump broken.
5.56	11.34	60	7	I.T. BOTHAM	c AND BOWLED	AKRAM	37	6	300	·	6	33	Mistimed hook - gentle return catch off splice.
11.36	3.13	179	8	J.E. EMBUREY	LBW	AKRAM	58	7	443	1	8	141	Late on breakback. His 4th fifty in Tests
3.15	4.52	78	9	N.A. FOSTER	RUN OUT (IJAZ)		29	9	512	·	3	63	Backed up - sent back - mid-off (direct hit)
4.26	(5.03)	37	10	P.H. EDMONDS	NOT OUT		24	·	·	·	3	27	
4.53	5.03	10	11	G.R. DILLEY	BOWLED	IMRAN	2	10	521	·	·	18	Off stump - padded up to inswinger.

* CAPTAIN † WICKET-KEEPER

EXTRAS b 1 lb 24 w 11 nb 16   52

1s 62s 1038 balls (inc 19 no balls)

TOTAL (169.5 OVERS - 713 MINUTES) 521   ALL OUT AT 5.03pm on 4th DAY.

14 OVERS 2 BALLS/HOUR
3.06 RUNS/OVER
50 RUNS/100 BALLS

BOWLER	O	M	R	W	%	HRS	OVERS	RUNS
IMRAN	41.5	8	129	6	3/4	1	15	35
AKRAM	43	12	83	3	3/4	2	13	25
QADIR	21	4	65	0	3/4	3	15	40
MUDASSAR	35	7	97	0	3/4	4	14	37
KAMAL	29	2	122	0	4/5	5	13	36
		25	1			6	16	60
	169.5	33	521	10		7	14	51
						8	14	37
						9	15	48
						10	14	54
						11	14	38

2nd NEW BALL taken at 5.33pm 3rd DAY
- ENGLAND 233-3 after 86 overs

RUNS	MINS	OVERS	LAST 50 (in mins)
50	95	22.1	95
100	180	43.0	85
150	260	61.0	80
200	317	74.2	57
250	376	90.1	59
300	440	104.4	64
350	510	121.4	70
400	574	136.5	64
450	637	151.2	63
500	690	164.3	53

STUMPS: 18-0 [7 OVERS / 27 MINUTES] BROAD 14* (31) ROBINSON 2* (11)
(2nd DAY) (421 BEHIND)

LUNCH: 72-0 [34 OVERS / 147 MIN] ROBINSON 26* (64) BROAD 39* (80)

TEA: 155-2 [63 OVERS / 367 MIN] ROBINSON 80* (171) GOWER 10* (17)

STUMPS: 273-5 [97 OVERS / 408 MIN] GATTING 38* (157) BOTHAM 16* (26)
(3rd DAY)

LUNCH: 364-6 [127 OVERS / 531 MIN] GATTING 88* (157) EMBUREY 11* (87)
75 BEHIND

TEA: 456-7 [155 OVERS / 651 MIN] GATTING 113* (217) FOSTER 5* (26)

ENGLAND'S LEAD: 82

WKT	PARTNERSHIP		RUNS	MINS
1st	Broad	Robinson	119	208
2nd	Robinson	Athey	13	27
3rd	Robinson	Gower	25	35
4th	Gower	Gatting	94	105
5th	Gatting	French	0	2
6th	Gatting	Botham	49	60
7th	Gatting	Emburey	143	189
8th	Gatting	Foster	41	50
9th	Foster	Edmonds	28	26
10th	Edmonds	Dilley	9	10
			521	

COMPILED by BILL FRINDALL

PAKISTAN 2ND INNINGS   (82 RUNS BEHIND ON FIRST INNINGS)

IN	OUT	MINS	No.	BATSMAN	HOW OUT	BOWLER	RUNS	WKT	TOTAL	6s	4s	BALLS	NOTES ON DISMISSAL
5.14	11.16	68	1	MUDASSAR NAZAR	BOWLED	DILLEY	10	1	47		1	48	Played outside ball that hit middle and off.
5.14	2.14	152	2	SHOAIB MOHD.	LBW	FOSTER	50	5	104		7	135	Played outside line of break-back.
11.18	1.48	57	3	MANSOOR AKHTAR	LBW	FOSTER	17	2	80		2	34	1000 F.C. RUNS. Ball kept low.
1.50	1.57	7	4	JAVED MIANDAD	C' EMBUREY	FOSTER	4	3	85		1	8	Defensive edge to 1st slip (away-seamer)
1.59	2.10	11	5	SALIM MALIK	C' AND BOWLED	BOTHAM	17	4	104		4	14	Superb reaction catch - right-handed falling to right.
2.12	2.35	23	6	IJAZ AHMED	BOWLED	BOTHAM	11	6	116		1	18	Leg stump - behind legs.
2.16	4.55	128	7	IMRAN KHAN *	LBW	FOSTER	37		204		5	94	Front foot - pushed outside line.
2.37	3.40	52	8	SALIM YOUSUF†	C' GATTING	EDMONDS	17	7	156		1	44	Drove to short extra-cover.
4.00	4.15	15	9	WASIM AKRAM	C' EDMONDS	DILLEY	6	8	165		1	18	Edged forward push to gully - waist-high catch
4.17	5.01	44	10	ABDUL QADIR	RUN OUT (FOSTER/FRENCH)		20	10	205		2	26	Attempted 2nd run to backward square-leg (superb fielding)
4.57	(5.01)	4	11	MOHSIN KAMAL	NOT OUT		0					4	

* CAPTAIN † WICKET-KEEPER

EXTRAS   b - lb 13   w 1   nb 2   16   4 25s 443 balls (inc 2 nb)

TOTAL (73.3 OVERS - 288 MINUTES) 205 ALL OUT at 5.01 pm on 5th DAY

15 OVERS 2 BALLS/HOUR
2.78 RUNS/OVER
46 RUNS/100 BALLS

BOWLER	O	M	R	W	Hrs	OVERS	RUNS
FOSTER	27	7	59	4	1	17	43
DILLEY	18	3	53	2	2	15	36
EMBUREY	4	1	3	0	3	15	39
BOTHAM	20.3	4	66	2	4	15	46
EDMONDS	4	1	11	1		13	1
	73.3	15	205	10			

	RUNS	MINS	OVERS	LAST 50 (in mins)
	50	75	20.4	75
	100	146	39.1	71
	150	218	56.5	72
	200	279	71.4	61

STUMPS: 38-0 (4th DAY) [15 OVERS 51 MINUTES | MUDASSAR 6* SHOAIB 32*]

LUNCH: 79-1 [32 OVERS 118 MINUTES | SHOAIB 49* (118) AKHTAR 16* (49')]

TEA: 156-7 [59.3 OVERS 227 MIN | IMRAN 21* (73')]

WKT	PARTNERSHIP		RUNS	MINS
1st	Mudassar	Shoaib	47	68
2nd	Shoaib	Akhtar	33	57
3rd	Shoaib	Miandad	5	7
4th	Shoaib	Malik	19	11
5th	Shoaib	Ijaz	0	2
6th	Ijaz	Imran	12	19
7th	Imran	Yousuf	40	52
8th	Imran	Akram	9	15
9th	Imran	Qadir	39	38
10th	Qadir	Kamal	1	4
			205	

COMPILED by BILL FRINDALL

ENGLAND 2ND INNINGS   REQUIRING 124 TO WIN OFF 18 OVERS (6.9 RUNS/OVER)

IN	OUT	MINS	No.	BATSMAN	HOW OUT	BOWLER	RUNS	WKT	TOTAL	6s	4s	BALLS	NOTES ON DISMISSAL
5.12	5.35	23	1	B.C. BROAD	C' MUDASSAR	IMRAN	30	1	37		5	23	Fended short ball to gully.
5.12	5.39	27	2	R.T. ROBINSON	C' IMRAN	AKRAM	4	2	39			10	Hooked to mid-on.
5.37	6.04	27	3	D.I. GOWER	BOWLED	IMRAN	18	4	72		2	15	Yorked.
5.41	5.48	7	4	I.T. BOTHAM	C' KAMAL	AKRAM	6	3	53		1	7	Top-edged swat at bouncer - skier to long-leg.
5.50	6.08	18	5	M.W. GATTING*	RUN OUT (IJAZ)		8	5	73		1	10	Backing up - extra-cover's return broke middle stump.
6.06	(6.44)	38	6	C.W.J. ATHEY	NOT OUT		14				1	20	
6.10	6.38	28	7	J.E. EMBUREY	RUN OUT (AKHTAR/YOUSUF)		20	6	108	1	1	18	Athey refused 2nd run to mid-wicket (1st ball of final over)
6.40	6.41	1	8	P.H. EDMONDS	RUN OUT (AKRAM)		0	7	108			2	Athey refused ultra-short run - beaten by bowler's throw.
6.42	(6.44)	2	9	B.N. FRENCH †	NOT OUT		1					1	
			10										
			11										

* CAPTAIN † WICKET-KEEPER

EXTRAS   b - lb 7   w 1   nb -   8   1s 1s 106 balls.

TOTAL (17.4 OVERS - 92 MINUTES) 109-7

11 OVERS 3 BALLS/HOUR
6.16 RUNS/OVER
102 RUNS/100 BALLS

BOWLER	O	M	R	W	Hrs	OVERS	RUNS
IMRAN KHAN	9	0	61	2	1	12	74
WASIM AKRAM	8.4	0	41	2		7	3
	17.4	0	109	7			

	RUNS	MINS	OVERS	LAST 50 (in mins)
	50	34	7.0	34
	100	77	15.4	43

MATCH DRAWN

MATCH AWARD : M.W. GATTING
(Adjudicator: R.D. JACKMAN)

WKT	PARTNERSHIP		RUNS	MINS
1st	Broad	Robinson	37	23
2nd	Robinson	Gower	2	2
3rd	Gower	Botham	14	7
4th	Gower	Gatting	19	18
5th	Gatting	Athey	1	2
6th	Athey	Emburey	35	28
7th	Athey	Edmonds	0	1
8th	Athey	French	1*	2
			109	

COMPILED by BILL FRINDALL

The Fifth Test at the Oval

Trevor Bailey

Victory at The Oval was the only way England could square the series and end an unprecedented run of disasters at home, whereas a draw would be sufficient for Imran Khan to become the first captain to win a rubber for Pakistan in England. Although the odds favoured the tourists, they had shown at Edgbaston that their batting lacked experience, and that they could panic if put under sufficient pressure. However, the record of Mike Gatting's attack that summer hardly suggested that it was likely to dismiss the opposition twice. Can England ever before have gone into the Fifth Test with five bowlers whose combined haul in first-class cricket amounted to only 164 wickets? It was made up as follows:

> Foster in 495 overs had captured 68 wickets at 19.57 each
> Dilley in 212 overs had captured 29 wickets at 22.58 each
> Botham in 197 overs had captured 29 wickets at 36.35 each
> Emburey in 316 overs had captured 21 wickets at 31.66 each
> Edmonds in 420 overs had captured 29 wickets at 33.58 each

In these circumstances it was difficult to understand why the selectors left out Neil Radford. He may not be much better than a fine county seamer, but he had taken more wickets for Worcestershire than had Dilley and Botham together for Worcester, and for fewer runs, so by the time Pakistan had passed the 700-mark his omission had become completely incomprehensible. True, there are obvious advantages in fielding a balanced attack of three seamers and two contrasting spinners rather than a quartet of pacemen, especially on a pitch which is expected to provide some help to slow bowlers. However, the spinners need to be wicket-takers and at that juncture Emburey had not captured any, and Edmonds had only four in the series.

The Massacre

Having called correctly, Imran Khan chose to take strike on a benign pitch which was lacking in pace, but did have an even bounce. Rather unexpectedly, the tourists began brightly with a flurry of attacking strokes, which lasted until they lost both Ramiz Raja and Mansoor Akhtar for 14 and 5. This was to be the only time when for a brief period England were in a better position. After that the Pakistan batsmen took firm, and eventually absolute, control. The rest of the first day belonged mainly to Mudassar, who contributed a sensible 70, and Miandad, who scored a most impressive century and was still there at stumps with Malik. The outlook for England had looked grim before lunch, as Mike Gatting had used all five members of his attack without seriously inconveniencing the opposition, but it was to become steadily worse. Forster, who had been below his best, retired with a bad back after only 12 overs and was not to bowl again in the match. Emburey, usually a model of accuracy, was wayward in both length and line, and in the final session Dilley limped off with a slightly injured ankle.

On the second day Pakistan ruthlessly extinguished any slight hope of an England victory by amassing 616 for 6, and, to make matters worse, the three wickets which fell owed little to the bowling. The inexperienced Malik, after a prolonged struggle in the 'nervous 90s' relaxed after completing his century and paid the penalty. Miandad, who made a superb 260, was more a victim of fatigue than of Dilley, while Imran Khan ran himself out, but not before he had become the third centurian, something which had looked probable from the moment he had strolled majestically to the crease.

Although the absence of Foster, who had been easily England's most impressive bowler throughout the series, weakened their attack, it has to be admitted that the remaining four were disappointing; indeed, Dilley, until he again limped off in the final session, was the only one who looked like beating the bat. What I found surprising throughout this batting massacre, which continued well into the third day, was the lack of imagination. None of the England bowlers attempted anything different. Surely it would have been worth Emburey trying a few overs from round the wicket, or at least using the crease to vary the angle? Edmonds might have experimented with a spell from over the wicket into the rough, while the two seamers simply kept plugging away, not too accurately, at the off-stump. The Pakistan batsmen were very strong off their legs and punched through the on-side anything that strayed off line. It might have paid, and would at least have made a change, to have reinforced the on-side field and attacked Pakistan's strength by aiming to hit the leg-stump. The seamers' only two ploys seemed to be a well-disguised slower ball from Dilley, and a very slow bouncer by Botham which was intended to induce a mishook, a result which became less probable as the match progressed.

On the third morning Ijaz Ahmed, surely destined to become an outstanding batsman, continued to plunder the bowling which, apart from Dilley's efforts, had become moribund. Botham by this time was little more than medium pace and was to gain the unwelcome distinction of being the first England bowler to concede over 200 runs in an innings, but what made it worse, and exposed the limitations of their attack, was that he was costing more than four runs per over. Imran might possibly have declared, if the umpires had not offered his batsmen the opportunity to come off for bad light, which they rejected. The stupidity of this particular law was again exposed by the way the ball was still dispatched to all parts of the ground. By passing 700 Pakistan gained a considerable psychological advantage and, in Abdul Qadir, they had the joker to exploit it.

The Surrender

Having experienced the unpleasantness of opening the innings for England, and knowing a total in excess of 400 was required to avoid the follow-on, I did not underestimate the task confronting Mike Gatting and company, if they were to save the match. Fortunately the pitch was still slow and docile, although it did look rather different when Imran and Akram launched their initial assault with the new ball in which Broad was brilliantly caught off an outswinger in the first over and England went in to take an uncomfortable lunch at 0 for 1. In the afternoon wrist spin-bowling combined with technical batting deficiencies accounted for three more wickets. However, a professional stand by Gatting and Botham, aided by an early closure for bad light, prevented further disaster. The outlook was still grim, with the score-board reading 144 for 4, two days remaining and another 365 required to avoid the follow-on.

When play was resumed on the Monday Gatting and Botham managed, but only just, to negotiate a brilliant spell of fast bowling, while from the other end Qadir weaved his spells. It was the little leg-spinner who was to account for both batsmen and also to dismiss a hypnotised French. By lunch the innings was in ruins and, although Emburey delayed the inevitable with an assortment of forward pushes, sweeps and cuts to reach an unusual fifty, England were all out for 232. The main destroyer had been Qadir, who had bemused and baffled with his wrist spin, which the batsmen had seldom encountered. His seven wickets for 96 were his best figures in a Test and illustrated the value of this style of bowling, even on a 'featherbed'.

The Escape
England followed on knowing that they had to show considerably more application if they were to avoid an innings defeat. Moxon and Broad began uncertainly against the new ball, but despite much playing and missing managed to survive. Moxon was the first to depart, flicking unwisely at an off-break from Tauseef, and although Broad continued to defend stubbornly, he lost both Robinson and Gower to Qadir before the close.

Could England hold out for six hours on what was still a docile pitch? It really all depended upon Broad, Gatting, Botham and Emburey, as one could not help feeling that even a weary Qadir would be able to dispose of the tail without too much trouble. There were three things in England's favour. First, the Pakistan attack was reduced to virtually three bowlers. Akram was in hospital with appendi-citis; Mudassar was ineffective in these conditions, and both spinners were very tired from their efforts on the previous day. What England needed was a solid start and a little luck. That is exactly what they enjoyed, as Gatting was dropped in the slips off Imran at the outset and then Broad and his captain remained until mid-morning. Although Qadir eventually dismissed the tall left-hander, this was his last success. Gatting found another ideal partner in Botham who, in the unaccustomed role of a defender, simply wore down the attack with the forward defensive combined with an astute use of his front pad.

Once they had negotiated the new ball in the afternoon with danger threatening from only one end, a draw became favourite and the final session was no more than a formality. Gatting finished with an undefeated 150 and Botham's half-century, although much the slowest of his career, was a masterly defensive exercise.

From a commentator's point of view, apart from the joy of seeing a leg-spinner not only in action for long periods, but also taking wickets, it was not a memorable Test. However, Bill Frindall enjoyed himself enormously as Pakistan in their massive total broke record after record. The match lacked the most important ingredient of a Test: sudden changes of fortune. From lunchtime on the second day, if not before, it was obvious that there were only two possible results. Before teatime on the last day there was only one outcome, a gallant, but nonetheless dull draw. In addition, the pitch lacked life, and as this also applied to some of the bowling, batting became too easy and there were rather too many runs. However *TMS* was fortunate in having a constant stream of visitors to our box which ranged from the great decision-makers of our land to representatives from the world of sport and entertainment.

In the first category there was god of the airwaves, Duke Hussey, chairman of the BBC, accompanied by several suitable seraphs. Next in order of rank was the president of the Surrey County Cricket Club, 'Big Al', while the House of Commons provided two ardent cricket-lovers, Michael Marshal and Robert Atkins. From the world of soccer came Gary Lineker, with his highly-developed instinct for putting the ball into the back of the net, and from rugby that true British Lion, Chris Rea. We were constantly inviting Leslie Crowther 'to come on up', and 'Goodies' Johnston had an especially entertaining chat on various aspects of cricket, both in England and Australia, with our Saturday morning guest, whose name escapes me, but 'Scccchhhh . . .', you must know who.

PAKISTAN 1ST INNINGS - ENGLAND (5TH TEST) at KENNINGTON OVAL, LONDON on 6,7,8,10,11 AUGUST, 1987.

IN	OUT	MINS	No	BATSMAN	HOW OUT	BOWLER	RUNS	WKT	TOTAL	6s	4s	BALLS	NOTES ON DISMISSAL TOSS: PAKISTAN.
11.00	2.34	174	1	MUDASSAR NAWAZ	C¹ MOXON	BOTHAM	73	3	148	·	8	142	Edged to 2nd slip.
11.00	11.40	40	2	RAMIZ RAJA	BOWLED	BOTHAM	14	1	40	·	2	25	off stump - inswinger through 'gate' - driving
11.42	11.53	11	3	MANSOOR AKHTAR	C¹ FRENCH	DILLEY	5	2	45	·	1	10	Edged outswinger to 'keeper
11.55	5.10	613	4	JAVED MIANDAD	C¹ and BOWLED	DILLEY	260	5	573	1	28	520	6000 RUNS (when 9) (15™ = TEST (1™ v ENG) (4 × 200) Mistimed slower ball (on run)
2.36	12.23	268	5	SALIM MALIK	C¹ GOWER	BOTHAM	102	4	382	·	6	238	(6™ = TESTS (2nd = ENG) Mistimed square-cut - chest-high to cover
12.25	5.40	252	6	IMRAN KHAN*	RUN OUT (BOTHAM)		118	6	601	1	11	200	(4™ = TESTS (1™ = ENG) Ijaz called him for 4th run to dp 3rd Man.
5.12	12.31	139	7	IJAZ AHMED	C¹ MOXON	DILLEY	69	8	707	·	9	98	Drove to wide mid-off
5.42	12.15	93	8	SALIM YOUSUF†	C¹ and BOWLED	DILLEY	42	7	690	·	4	68	Low right-handed catch from mistimed drive.
12.17	12.42	25	9	WASIM AKRAM	C¹ BOTHAM	DILLEY	5	10	708	·	·	15	Gloved hook to 2nd slip.
12.33	12.35	2	10	ABDUL QADIR	C¹ MOXON	DILLEY	0	9	707	·	·	4	Edged lifting ball to 3rd slip.
12.37	(12.42)	5	11	TAUSIF AHMED	NOT OUT		0			·	·	3	

* CAPTAIN   † WICKET-KEEPER

| EXTRAS | b 2 lb 18 w - nb - | 20 | 2s 69s 1323 balls |

UMPIRES:-
D.J. CONSTANT
K.E. PALMER

TOTAL (220.3 OVERS · 820 MINUTES) 708 ALL OUT AT 12.42 pm on 3RD DAY

RECORD TOTAL BY PAKISTAN; 2ND HIGHEST TOTAL v ENGLAND

16 OVERS 0 BALLS/HOUR
3.21 RUNS/OVER
53 RUNS/100 BALLS

BOWLER	O	M	R	W
DILLEY	47.3	10	154	6
FOSTER	12	3	32	0
BOTHAM	52	7	217	3
EMBUREY	61	0	143	0
EDMONDS	32	8	97	0
GATTING	10	2	18	0
MOXON	6	2	27	0
	220.3	42	708	—

2ND NEW BALL TAKEN at 4.56 pm (1st day)
- PAKISTAN 253-3 after 86.2 overs
3RD NEW BALL TAKEN at 4.25 pm 2nd day
- PAKISTAN 525-4 after 174.2 overs

HRS	OVERS	RUNS
1	14	47
2	18	48
3	16	59
4	18	48
5	21	55
6	14	40
7	14	53
8	18	56
9	16	34
10	19	60
11	14	67
12	15	49
13	14	70

RUNS	MINS	OVERS	LAST 50 (in mins)
50	67	15.3	67
100	128	34.0	61
150	178	47.1	50
200	237	65.2	59
250	297	86.2	60
300	364	102.0	67
350	417	114.5	53
400	445	128.2	48
450	555	154.1	90
500	593	166.0	38
550	646	179.3	53
600	689	191.0	43

LUNCH: 95-2 [32 OVERS / 120 MIN] MUDASSAR 45* (120) MIANDAD 25* (65')

TEA: 206-3 [67 OVERS / 242 MIN] MIANDAD 82* (187') MALIK 23* (66')

STUMPS: 297-3 [101 OVERS / 361 MIN] MIANDAD 131* (306') (1ST DAY) MALIK 64* (195')

LUNCH: 406-4 [133 OVERS / 481 MIN] MIANDAD 189* (426') IMRAN 12* (35')

TEA: 500-4 [168 OVERS / 599 MIN] MIANDAD 243* (544') IMRAN 51* (153')

STUMPS: 616-6 [197 OVERS / 718 MIN] IJAZ 22* (48') (2ND DAY) YOUSUF 6* (18')

R	M	W50	R	M	W50
650	744	202.4	55	700	804	217.1	60

BOTHAM (217) CONCEDED RECORD BY ENGLAND BOWLER

WKT	PARTNERSHIP		RUNS	MINS
1st	Mudassar	Ramiz	40	40
2nd	Mudassar	Akhtar	5	11
3rd	Mudassar	Miandad	103	119
4th	Miandad	Malik	234†	268
5th	Miandad	Imran	191	222
6th	Imran	Ijaz	28	28
7th	Ijaz	Yousuf	89‡	93
8th	Ijaz	Akram	17	14
9th	Akram	Qadir	0	0
10th	Akram	Tausif	1	5

† PAKISTAN 4TH WICKET RECORD v ENGLAND
‡ PAKISTAN 7TH WICKET RECORD v ENGLAND

COMPILED BY BILL FRINDALL.

ENGLAND v PAKISTAN 1987

ENGLAND FIRST INNINGS
(IN REPLY TO PAKISTAN'S 708 ALL OUT - 509 TO AVOID FOLLOW-ON)

IN	OUT	MINS	No.	BATSMAN	HOW OUT	BOWLER	RUNS	WKT	TOTAL	6s	4s	BALLS	NOTES ON DISMISSAL
12·54	12·56	2	1	B.C. BROAD	c' YOUSUF	IMRAN	0	1	0	·	·	4	Edged outswinger low to 'keeper's left - diving catch
12·54	2·31	60	2	M.D. MOXON	c' MIANDAD	QADIR	8	2	32	·	·	45	Edged off-drive to slip
12·58	2·54	79	3	R.T. ROBINSON	BOWLED	QADIR	30	3	54	·	5	62	Missed pull at long-hop.
2·33	3·35	62	4	D.I GOWER	BOWLED	TAUSIF	28	4	78	·	4	39	Played on - cutting
2·50	11·49	164	5	M.W. GATTING *	c' IMRAN	QADIR	61	6	166	·	10	136	Drove to mid-on.
3·37	11·39	113	6	I.T. BOTHAM	BOWLED	QADIR	34	5	165	·	3	82	Played on - drove outside half-volley (googly)
11·41	2·29	128	7	J.E. EMBUREY	c' MALIK	QADIR	53	10	232	1	6	115	1000 RUNS → TEST DOUBLE. Cut hard to 2nd slip
11·51	12·26	35	8	B.N. FRENCH †	c' MALIK	QADIR	1	7	184	·	·	29	Skier to cover - edged off-drive.
12·28	1·50	42	9	N.A. FOSTER	c' IJAZ	TAUSIF	4	8	198	·	·	52	Edged off-break via pad to forward short-leg.
1·51	2·15	24	10	P.H. EDMONDS	LBW	QADIR	2	9	223	·	·	26	Beaten by googly.
2·17	(2·29)	12	11	G.R. DILLEY	NOT OUT		0			·	·	11	-

* CAPTAIN † WICKET-KEEPER

EXTRAS b 4 lb 3 w 1 nb 3 = 11   1st 28 601 BALLS (inc. 3 no balls)

TOTAL (99·4 OVERS - 369 MINUTES) 232   All out at 2.29 on 4th day.

(476 BEHIND ON FIRST INNINGS)

16 OVERS 1 BALLS/HOUR
2·32 RUNS/OVER
38 RUNS/100 BALLS

BOWLER	O	M	R	W	NB/W	HRS	OVERS	RUNS
IMRAN	18	2	39	1	·	1	15	32
AKRAM	14	2	37	0	1/1	2	14	46
QADIR	44·4	15	96	7	·/2	3	16	54
TAUSIF	23	9	53	2	·	4	15	33
						5	16	27
			7			6	20	31
	99·4	28	232	10				

* HIS BEST ANALYSIS IN TESTS
2ND NEW BALL not taken.

RUNS	MINS	OVERS	LAST 50 (IN MINS)
50	79	20·3	79
100	142	34·2	63
150	207	51·4	65
200	338	89·2	131

LUNCH: 0-1   [2 OVERS] MOXON 0* (9') [9 MIN] ROBINSON 0* (5')

TEA: 81-4   [31 OVERS] GATTING 11* (51) [130 MIN] BOTHAM 1* (4')

STUMPS: 144-4 (3RD DAY)   [50 OVERS] GATTING 50* (115) [200 MIN] BOTHAM 23* (71')

LUNCH: 193-7   [84 OVERS] EMBUREY 24* (79) [316 TO AVOID FOLLOW-ON] [320 MIN] FOSTER 1* (32')

WKT	PARTNERSHIP		RUNS	MINS
1st	Broad	Moxon	0	2
2nd	Moxon	Robinson	32	56
3rd	Robinson	Gower	22	21
4th	Gower	Gatting	24	39
5th	Gatting	Botham	87	113
6th	Gatting	Emburey	1	8
7th	Emburey	French	18	35
8th	Emburey	Foster	14	42
9th	Emburey	Edmonds	25	24
10th	Emburey	Dilley	9	12
			232	

COMPILED BY BILL FRINDALL

ENGLAND 2ND INNINGS
FOLLOWING ON 476 RUNS BEHIND

IN	OUT	MINS	No.	BATSMAN	HOW OUT	BOWLER	RUNS	WKT	TOTAL	6s	4s	BALLS	NOTES ON DISMISSAL
2·42	12·14	250	1	B.C. BROAD	c' IJAZ	QADIR	42	4	139	·	3	204	Edged off-break (to him) via pad to diving silly point
2·42	4·10	66	2	M.D. MOXON	c' YOUSUF	TAUSIF	15	1	22	·	1	57	Edged glance at off-break - legside catch.
4·12	4·38	26	3	R.T. ROBINSON	c' AKRAM	QADIR	10	2	40	·	1	24	Top-edged sweep - remarkable diving catch (bkwd sq. leg)
4·40	5·41	61	4	D.I. GOWER	c' MUDASSAR	QADIR	34	3	89	·	3	58	Edged leg-break via pad to forward short-leg.
5·43	(5·28)	343	5	M.W. GATTING *	NOT OUT		150			·	21	303	
12·16	(5·28)	250	6	I.T. BOTHAM	NOT OUT		51			·	9	209	
			7										
			8										
			9										
			10										
			11										

* CAPTAIN † WICKET-KEEPER

EXTRAS b 4 lb 5 w 1 nb 3 = 13   - 38 855 BALLS (inc. 3 no balls)

TOTAL (142 OVERS - 502 MINUTES) 315-4

16 OVERS 5 BALLS/HOUR
2·21 RUNS/OVER
36 RUNS/100 BALLS

BOWLER	O	M	R	W	NB/W	HRS	OVERS	RUNS
IMRAN	26·3	8	59	0	·	1	16	17
AKRAM	6	3	3	0	1/·	2	18	40
QADIR	53	21	115	3	·	3	17	39
TAUSIF	46·3	15	98	1	·/·	4	17	28
MUDASSAR	6	0	21	0	1/5	5	19	50
MIANDAD	4	2	10	0	·/·	6	14	36
			9			7	20	48
	142	49	315	4		8	15	37

2ND NEW BALL taken at 1·52pm on 5th day
- ENGLAND 175-4 after 89 overs

RUNS	MINS	OVERS	LAST 50 (IN MINS)
50	110	31·1	110
100	198	56·0	88
150	267	75·4	69
200	332	94·4	65
250	399	114·4	67
300	485	137·1	86

TEA: 17-0   [15 OVERS] 459 [58 MIN] BEHIND   BROAD 6* MOXON 10*

STUMPS: 95-3 (4TH DAY)   [50 OVERS] 381 [176 MIN] BEHIND   BROAD 26* (1/2) GATTING 5* (11)

LUNCH: 170-4   [86 OVERS] 306 [296 MIN] BEHIND   GATTING 61* (112) BOTHAM 1* (6')

TEA: 257-4   [120 OVERS] 219 [416 MIN] BEHIND   GATTING 121* (147) BOTHAM 25* (114')

MATCH DRAWN

MAN OF THE MATCH : JAVED MIANDAD
(Adjudicator : R. ILLINGWORTH)

SERIES AWARDS : M.W. GATTING and IMRAN KHAN

WKT	PARTNERSHIP		RUNS	MINS
1st	Broad	Moxon	22	66
2nd	Broad	Robinson	18	26
3rd	Broad	Gower	49	61
4th	Broad	Gatting	50	91
5th	Gatting	Botham	176*	250
6th				
7th				
8th				
9th				
10th			315	

COMPILED BY BILL FRINDALL

A Dip in the Post Bag

Peter Baxter

The vast amount of hot air generated in the commentary boxes round the country as rain fell persistently in the soggy summer of 1987 gave rise in turn to plenty of letters. We reckon ourselves very fortunate in our correspondents, who get thoroughly involved in, and sometimes quite heated about, the various topics of conversation which arise. Of course I receive a good many which criticise a commentator, but usually saying that the writer likes all the team except for one individual, and people can get surprisingly vitriolic about their dislikes. The likes and dislikes, however, even out to a remarkable extent.

We are very fortunate also on *Test Match Special* to get a number of very friendly letters, particularly at the end of the season, just saying 'thank you'. No one gets more of this – or, indeed of any – genre than Brian Johnston. His 75th birthday produced a flood of good wishes, from such as Dorothy Bond of Bridport who promised to repeat them in five years' time. A much younger listener, Joanne Drake, wrote from Sutton Coldfield with great concern at rumours of Brian's impending retirement from the commentary team. 'It wouldn't be the same without old Johnners', she said. Amen to that, but while he is still enjoying it I hope we can hang on to him.

Brian seems to inspire that kind of affection and letters that start, as John Knowles from Leamington Spa's did, 'Good old Johnners!' He ended with the PS: 'Don't even *think* of retiring.' But the point of his letter was to say that he had just, on a climbing expedition to K2 in Pakistan, come to appreciate the significance of those words, '. . . and we welcome World Service listeners'. The two quarter-hour sessions a day for those who cannot tune into the constant Special Overseas Cricket Transmission are all too short. John Knowles' problem was that, as the owner of the short wave radio, he was the one who had to break the news of England's defeat to his jubilant Pakistani colleagues.

Some of Brian's correspondents are guests of Her Majesty's prison service. One of these wrote particularly enthusiastically from Bristol to say how he had converted one of his mates 'inside' to cricket with the aid of *TMS*. I suppose we all like to have a captive audience.

It is traditional for letters to come in promoting the cause of a player whose performances in county cricket seem to have been overlooked by the selectors. (Some listeners seem to think *we* are selectors!) In 1987 the praises were sung from Lancashire of Graeme Fowler; from Southampton of the Smith brothers and from

Worcestershire of Tim Curtis, among others. Several people wrote in surprise at the dropping of Jack Richards, who, they felt, had not done anything wrong.

It was nice to be congratulated on some of the selections in the commentary box. Robin Jackman's appearance produced some of this reaction; someone else warned, 'Don't let television take Jack Bannister'. Mushtaq Mohammed – 'Mushy' to one and all – was as popular as he was on his previous appearances. Mrs Vicky Poynting wrote from a Lincolnshire vicarage to say that she and her husband had enjoyed listening to Mushy's 'gentle voice – always wise, never criticising – well, perhaps a little, but in the nicest possible way'.

Mushy was very useful to us as a guide with identification and a tutor in pronunciation. Abdul Qadir's name raised the usual arguments. The Mushtaq version of 'Kardher' was rejected by Laurence Carrington-Windo, for instance, 'Abdul Carter!' he wrote, 'Surely this must cast severe doubts over his nationality'. Some of our television colleagues, we were told, were pronouncing it 'Kadear'. We asked Qadir himself. 'Call me Abdul,' was his solution.

The weather itself was, of course, a great talking-point. We always seem to mention the 'Manchester weather' as if it is always as bad as it was this year. R. Hayden of Stockport was one of those who sprang to its defence, pointing out that if the Second Test had been at Old Trafford there would have been play on all five days. Alec Balfe-Mitchell, a minister in the south-west Manchester group of churches, wrote to identify for us one of the landmarks that we spent so much time looking at on the rain-misted sky-line, the 134-year-old spire of St Mary's, Hulme; at 241 feet the tallest church spire in the Diocese of Manchester. Mr Balfe-Mitchell included the sort of joke which appeals to Brian:

Q: Where in the Bible is reference to cricket to be found?
A: Old Testament prophets referred to removal of the Baals!

Watching the rain reminded Trevor Bailey of a 20-minute commentary by John Arlott several years ago at Lord's on the removal of the covers. It was certainly one of the most entertaining pieces of broadcasting I have heard, but sadly the recording was stopped when the play stopped for rain.

More even than rain, bad light is a topic that never ceases to arouse passions. Malcolm Jones wrote from the West Midlands to complain about the tactical nature of decisions to accept offers of bad light. It is a point often discussed on *TMS* and I think we are unanimous that bad light offers are made much too early.

Another umpiring decision which caused plenty of discussion was the dismissal of Chris Broad at Headingley, caught off a glove which was not, apparently, in contact with the bat. I was interested to see afterwards that Broad himself was not in favour of the 'third umpire with a playback' notion. Benjamin Peret wrote from London to defend the man in the hot seat, umpire David Shepherd. He felt the television replays had been unfair and he even suggested that Broad might have been out 'handled the ball'. I don't think he was, but there was an opposite view from Maurice Peberdy from Loughborough, anyway, suggesting that a batsman should never be out caught off a glove. Fred, he suggested, would never agree.

The Headingley Test was all over just 20 minutes into the fourth day, prompting from Martin Reppion of Brighouse the suggestion of a 'last day cup' for such occasions. A fine theory, but I cannot see it finding much favour with the players. England had also been somewhat hampered in that Headingley match by injury and several people suggested that substitutes should be allowed to take full part in the match. The trouble would be that there would inevitably be 'tactical' injuries as the situation changed and a different type of batsman or bowler was needed. We have seen the present system abused on occasion since the law about specialist fieldsmen substitutions was changed.

A number of listeners wrote after England's first innings at Headingley to point out the coincidence of the number of 13s in the scorecard. The wickets fell: 2–13, 3–13, 4–31 (reversed), 5–31, 7–113, 8–133, 9–133, 10–136. Even the sixth wicket fell at 85 and 8 plus 5, I am reliably informed, equals 13. It was certainly not a lucky Test for England.

Commentators' errors are, of course, pounced on with great delight, although I think R.S. King, who asked of Henry 'Does one leave by an entrance?', was being a little less than charitable. R.P. Amey of Worthing heard Christopher say 'Javed Miandad, still wearing a sleeveless sweater under his white crash helmet . . . ' and wanted to know if someone had pulled the wool over his eyes.

Strange cricketing incidents are often reported to us, like the match between Chevening and Biggin Hill 30 years ago. Roger Leavens told us that Chevening easily overhauled their opponents' score of 32 without losing a wicket. 'Nothing unusual in that,' he wrote, 'but one of the openers did not face a single ball throughout the innings.' From Yorkshire we heard from Paul Hatfield, who had seen a team-mate given out caught off his head. 'Well,' said the umpire, 'it sounded like wood!' And in Wiltshire S.T. Woolaway's office team had to press their secretary, Christine Treble, into service to make up an XI. After questions such as 'Is the ball hard?' and 'Which end of the racquet do I hold?' she was put in to bat at 11. She put them all to shame by being joint top scorer with eight.

The end of the Edgbaston Test, when the players came off with a possible two balls to go, caused a flurry of letter-writing. It was certainly an anti-climactic end, but play only continues on the last day after 5.30 if either captain feels he can achieve a win. A positive result had become an impossibility, but I did feel the decision was a bad bit of public relations after such a dramatic last day. Another idea that has been aired from time to time, and was again in 1987 by M.J. Baker from Bath, is the alternating of choice of innings in a series after a toss at the start of the First Test. I think most people would regret the passing of such a part of the game as the toss and that would surely lead to considerable tactical team selections, with the result of the toss known in advance. Bumpers were again under attack, particularly from Herbert Woodward, who deplored the expression, 'a good bouncer'. He was in favour of a line across the pitch, any ball pitching in the batsman's half being called a six or at least four byes. This, he felt, would eliminate his other hate, the helmet. It would also, of course, eliminate the hook shot.

G.N. Strothard of Thornbury, Bradford suggested that Ian Botham ought to finish his career with ten or 12 years as a wicketkeeper. 'Maybe then,' he said, 'we will all be convinced that Ian is the finest cricketer of all time.' It sounds like just the sort of challenge to appeal to the great man for a game or two, but I think he likes his bowling too much to make it permanent and he might well be the biggest 'keeper of all time.

The cakes we receive in the commentary box have become legendary. Headingley remains the cake capital of the Test match circuit, but at The Oval we received an appetising-looking cake from Gavin Simonsen in Preston. Appetising, that is, until we saw the wick in the top of each slice. It was a collection of six candles made by Gavin's firm.

I mentioned the pleasure of receiving congratulations for commentary selections, but nothing brought so many of these as our Saturday afternoon during the MCC Bicentenary match at Lord's when Rex Alston and Jim Swanton took to the airwaves again. Many of our listeners recalled hearing the two together for the first time in the 1940s and enjoyed the nostalgia of the occasion.

Finally let me return to Abdul Qadir. We have seen a similar parody before, but I enjoyed this version by R.G. Pearce of Camborne in Cornwall. His ballad was ten verses long and started:

> Oh the spin bowler's art
> Must come straight from the heart,
> Inspiring in batsmen much fear.
> And most cunning by far
> Is the man from Lahore,
> Called Abdul a bowl bowl Qadir.

(I think you can tell which version of the pronunciation Mr Pearce favours.) He went on to provide us with a poetic testimonial:

> For five days they fought,
> No ground given or sought,
> And the battle was heard through the land
> Thanks to those heroes all,
> Johnners, Mushy and Boil,
> Who talk on the radio band.
>
> All the best cricket books
> Record pulls, sweeps and hooks
> From the batsmen throughout history.
> But if you wish to know
> Who won this cricket show,
> You must listen to Radio 3.

The Bicentenary Match

First Day

Christopher Martin—Jenkins

It was a lovely start to the match. I had taken a personal interest in it for longer than most having been honoured to be a member of the MCC sub-committee which under Hubert Doggart's energetic chairmanship had planned the year's celebrations with this game as the centrepiece. Any doubts anyone retained about the interest in a match at Lord's not directly involving the home country were dissolved as the crowd began streaming in on a gloriously warm and sunny morning. They saw a hard-fought day's cricket on a perfect pitch for batting, the rehabilitation of Graham Gooch's international career and a sensational piece of fielding by Roger Harper.

I had a shorter journey than usual to the ground for my early morning broadcast on Radio 4, having spent the night with Brian and Pauline Johnston and various members of the clan Johnston including grandson Harry. I had been with Brian to the memorable eve-of-match dinner at the Guildhall. Doggart, Lord Home and Clive Lloyd had all spoken well and to rub shoulders with literally hundreds of wonderful cricketers in the majestic setting of the Guildhall was an experience not to be missed.

On my own table at the dinner were Ted Dexter, Steve Comacho from the West Indies, Joe Pamensky from South Africa and Alwyn Pichanek from Zimbabwe, all within easy range of conversation. Around the rest of the vast hall were many friends, not just celebrities but people one has played cricket with in MCC out matches and other wandering cricket. It was a perfect prologue to a game which began with Gatting winning the toss and making first use of Mick Hunt's beautiful pitch. How relieved Hunt and his staff must have felt to wake to such a lovely morning after the misery of losing three whole days of the Test match earlier in the season.

By the time the crowd were settling to their lunchtime picnics Gordon Greenidge was halfway to the hundred he was clearly determined to get. But after lunch he hit Abdul Qadir hard and high to Harper, who took the catch with great ease and the centre of the stage was taken instead by Graham Gooch. At first he trod there on tiptoes, apologetic after a relatively modest season for Essex, out of the England side and chosen for this match only as a reserve for the injured Martin

Gordon Greenidge with another example of how the reverse sweep can be played on *the way to his hundred at Lord's.*

Patrick Eagar

Crowe. Gradually he blossomed into the rosy-faced, upstanding, commanding Gooch of old, as much at home on the Lord's pitch as the village constable standing chatting beside his bike on the green.

It took a staggering bit of fielding by Harper to run Gooch out for 117. He drove hard back down the pitch from perhaps a yard in front of his popping crease. Harper swooped, stopped the ball and in the same movement flicked a lethal return throw over the stranded batsman on to the stumps. The analogy of the beached whale was hard to resist.

My son Robin and a team-mate from Cranleigh Prep School First XI had chosen the moment of Harper's sorcery to go to the loo and were behind a pillar at the crucial moment. The crowd's roar, a mixture of delight and amazement, told them what they had missed.

Gooch himself can seldom have been less disappointed to be out. He had made his point, as much to himself as anyone else, and none of the bowlers, Harper included, had looked like getting him in any orthodox way. My notes show that he was especially severe on Walsh, tapping him off his toes no fewer than five times in one spell to the New Mound Stand, packed as it was like a brand new cruise ship with people in holiday mood.

Harper was unlucky not to get Gatting as well before the close when the sturdy England captain, then 54 not out, drove him to deep mid-on where Homer, in the form of Javed Miandad, nodded. Gatting played very well, though not so well as he was to do next day. Rice, serious and combative in this match as ever he was for Nottinghamshire, got his head down and gave the bowlers nothing. His innings was entirely in tune with the mood of the day: non-frivolous, but immensely enjoyable. MCC, off 96 overs (completed 20 minutes late) were 291 for 4, Gatting 68 not out and Rice 14 not out. Off we went from Lord's to the *TMS* dinner in Broadcasting House.

Second Day
Fred Trueman

Fred Trueman toasts the two commentators who made their comeback at the Bicentenary match – Rex Alston and E.W. Swanton.

We arrived for the second day's play mostly in good condition after the previous evening's excellent commentators' dinner. We had entertained officials of the TCCB and MCC and were delighted also to be joined by two old friends, Rex Alston and Jim Swanton, who were to take to the airwaves again on Saturday.

That morning at Lord's it was apparent to me that Clive Rice, having replaced the injured Botham, meant to stamp his name on this game. It was probably the only time in his career that he would have a world stage on which to present his talents. So his common-sense innings of 59 not out did not surprise me. Meanwhile Mike Gatting, in prolific form, was taking toll of some wayward bowling by Imran Khan and Courtney Walsh. They bowled too short on such a good batting pitch and the shots off the back foot by Gatting and Rice were a delight to see. In the first ten overs of the day 55 runs came.

Gatting rattled his way to a superb 179 before many people, including myself, thought he was out caught behind the wicket. In fact the ball, which he had attempted to cut, had nicked the side of the off-stump and remarkably it was the leg bail that fell off and a couple of the close-to-the-wicket fielders even appealed for the catch, but the noise they had heard was the ball clipping the stump. At this point Gatting declared the MCC innings at 455 for 5. In a Test match with a side of such batting strength, Mike would probably have been looking for a total of about 650, but his declaration now was in the spirit of the festival occasion.

Also in the spirit of the celebrations was the stream of distinguished visitors to our commentary box. None was more welcome than Graeme Pollock. I was one of many who thought that he should have been invited to play in this match in the Rest of the World team. Politics had robbed the world of the chance to enjoy this great South African left-hander and I think it would have been a fitting tribute to a wonderful player and a very nice person to have given him this last first-class appearance at Lord's.

Two great Australian batsmen came up to the box together: Bill Brown, who talked to us of the hundreds he made in the 30s (as a boy I saw him at Bramall Lane in 1948); and Neil Harvey, a great left-handed batsman and magnificent cover fielder whom I played against on many occasions. Alan Davidson, that wonderful New South Wales and Australia all-rounder, came to see us and so did a cavalier character who bordered in his day on genius – Denis Compton. Jeffrey Stollmeyer, fine opening batsman and captain of the West Indies and now a quiet, authoritative administrator dropped in. Then we had an up and coming star; a man whose name will figure very prominently I believe in Test cricket in the future – Martin Crowe. Unfortunately he had had to withdraw from the MCC side with a broken thumb. Martin has already contributed so much to cricket in this country that it would have been a fitting moment for him to have walked out to represent MCC and we all wished him well for the future.

Our visitors provided us with a memorable day, but there was plenty of excitement on the field of play as well. As the Rest of the World started their reply, there was a very loud appeal from the first ball that Malcolm Marshall bowled to Sunil Gavaskar. But the lbw shout was turned down, much to the dismay of the MCC players. Thereafter the little man displayed his true class. He was 80 not out at the close of play and his innings, together with the superb fast bowling of Marshall, was the talking point as people left the ground. Marshall had bowled 11 overs, three of them maidens, and had taken two wickets for 14. The Rest of the World were 169 for 3 – 286 runs behind. The game was beautifully poised and the departing crowds were buzzing with expectation for the next day.

As we were leaving, however, came the news that Sunny Gavaskar had announced his retirement. It is always a sad moment when a great player announces his retirement and in this case it was the scorer of more runs and centuries in Test cricket than anyone. He had already in this innings given us a lesson in the art of batting against the fearsome bowling of Malcolm Marshall, and we felt there was more to come, though we were reminded that he had never made a century at Lord's.

And so we repaired to the garden and the hospitality of our old pal, Brian Johnston, just up the road. Surely no one in the world could have staged such a party so well or have attracted so many famous faces and old friends. It was a perfect way to end a great day's cricket.

Third Day

Brian Johnston

On the Friday of the match my wife Pauline and I had our annual supper party in our garden in St John's Wood. Try selecting a team from the following former Test players who were among the guests. If Denis Compton had remembered to come, it would have been an even better side! Note the strength of all-rounders in the 'squad': Jeff Stollmeyer, Tom Graveney, Neil Harvey, Keith Miller, Hubert Doggart, Ray Illingworth, Alan Davidson, Ray Lindwall, Colin Milburn, Raman Subba Row, Ted Dexter, Bob Wyatt, Trevor Bailey, Richie Benaud, Alan Smith, Fred Trueman.

I think George must be 12th Mann! Our timing was perfect. As the guests arrived Concorde flew overhead and I swear that it dipped its wings in salute. And the rain that had been threatening all evening held off until we had all finished our supper. It started lightly, but soon became a deluge. It must have rained all night: anyway it was pelting down at 5.30 a.m. when I woke up and it was still drizzling when I made my way to Lord's to talk to Cliff Morgan on *Sport on 4*.

I arrived at 8.30 a.m. and popped in to see Dickie Bird and David Shepherd in the Umpires' Room. They weren't too optimistic about the weather and the secretary of MCC, Lt-Col John Stephenson, said he had just recorded a message for the Prospects of Play service, saying play was unlikely before lunch. There were pools of water all over the ground but by 9 a.m. the sun had started to break through the clouds. Mick Hunt and his groundstaff were doing a great job with the whale, water-hop and motor mop. By the time *Sport on 4* finished the pools had begun to disappear, and the sun was becoming quite hot. Unbelievably, after several inspections by the umpires, it was announced that play would start at 11.30 a.m. The outfield was still very wet and had it been a Test match I'm sure they would not have started so soon. But it did prove a point. Although the fielders did occasionally slip and slide, and had to move warily, there was no danger of injury to them – the excuse always given for not starting Tests.

Gavaskar – 80 not out overnight – continued his fascinating duel with Malcolm Marshall and Richard Hadlee, and at least showed that he was human. He spent 17 minutes in the 90s before he reached his first ever hundred at Lord's. He was given a tremendous ovation. Nightwatchman Dujon had been caught by Gooch at third slip in the first over, and with Imran playing second fiddle the score at lunch was 264 for 4; Gavaskar 128, Imran 42. After lunch Imran took over and played some magnificent strokes, including two giant sixes into the pavilion. He was finally bowled by Shastri for a fine 82. Kapil Dev had a brief slog for 13 before being caught at long-off by Marshall off Emburey. This was Emburey's first wicket of the summer in big cricket.

Gavaskar continued to delight with his wonderfully correct and beautifully timed stroke-play. It looked as if he would get 200 in what he had said would be his last first-class match. But after stroking Shastri twice past extra cover he played a bit early and was caught and bowled by Shastri for 188. It was one of the greatest innings seen at Lord's, and the spectators rose as one to applaud and make sure that 'he was pavilioned in splendour'.

At tea it was 391 for 7 with Harper and Walsh together. But it then started to rain and the light became appalling. There was an hour and a quarter's delay and then out came the umpires with their white coats, although it was still very dark. There was a slight delay before MCC followed them out, no doubt because of the shock of being asked to play in such conditions.

But again a point was proved. So long as slow bowlers are used there is no 'risk of serious injury to the batsman' – the criterion by which Test umpires are asked to judge. In fact, it became obvious that it was the fielders who found it difficult to see. Harper and Walsh found it easy. They added 30 runs in 15 minutes, before rain finally put a stop to play for the day, with the Rest of the World 421 for 7 at which total Allan Border declared that evening.

But well done the umpires. Dickie Bird was nearly in tears as a result of the welcome given to him and David Shepherd as they returned to the pavilion. Members cheered, clapped and tried to shake them by the hand. What a contrast to that dreadful Saturday of the 1980 Centenary Test at Lord's!

Visitors continued to flow into our box. We asked Tom Graveney to explain why the Duke of Edinburgh had called Tom his 'rabbit' in an interview with me. The Duke had said he had got Tom caught at short leg, Tom says he was trying to hit a six and was caught at deep mid-wicket. Believe which version you like! The remaining two 'Ws' came together. What a pity the third 'W' – Sir Frank Worrell – died so young, aged only 43. He had done so much to weld the various islands into a West Indian team.

I asked Clyde Walcott if, when he was wicketkeeper in 1950, he was able to 'read' Sonny Ramadhin's leg-break. He replied that he couldn't always do so, but that it didn't really matter as Sonny himself seldom knew which ball he was going to bowl!

One of our many guests during the Bicentenary match – Clive Lloyd, manager of the Rest of the World side.

A unique cake for Brian on a unique occasion.

Everton Weekes' face was wreathed in a permanent smile, no doubt he was recalling some Grand Slam he had made in bridge, which he plays so well. He modestly demurred when Fred told him that his 90 at Lord's in 1957 on a bad wicket was one of the bravest innings Fred had ever seen.

Clive Lloyd made a sensible, if impracticable suggestion. He said that before every annual meeting of the ICC the captains of all the cricketing countries should meet to put forward their ideas for changes in laws and conditions. I am all in favour of any suggestion which will help the ICC come to any decision on anything!

A loud booming sound heralded the arrival of Frank Tyson, over here in England for a year to coach and teach French at Denstone College. We were so surprised at his hidden talent that we asked him to prove that he could speak French. As soon as he did so, there was the inevitable chorus from us all in the box: 'How wise not to attempt the French accent'. We asked him what had made him change to a short run, after he had taken 1 for 160 in the First Test at Brisbane in 1954. He replied that he had not changed, but reverted to a shorter run, which he had originally always used when he first bowled in first-class cricket. Anyway it worked, if you remember, as he proceeded to take 27 wickets in the next four Tests with the fastest bowling those present had ever seen.

Finally we were especially pleased that Sunil Gavaskar took the trouble to spend nearly half-an-hour talking to us. He must have been very tired after his long innings but was modest, friendly and amusing. I may be wrong but I thought I detected a slight uncertainty in his reply to my question about whether his decision to leave first-class cricket was final. He certainly confirmed that he had made the decision, but when asked if he might change his mind replied, 'Well, we are all human . . . ' He made two interesting choices when asked who was the best fast bowler and spinner he had ever played against. He plumped immediately for Andy Roberts and Derek Underwood.

So much for visiting Test players. But with all due respect to them the highlight of the day for us in the box was the return of Rex Alston and Jim Swanton, who gave a nostalgic *á deux* commentary for 24 minutes or so in the afternoon. Rex said that he had not given a radio commentary for 23 years but he did wonderfully well. He kept up with the play, identified the players and described the action as if he had never been away. What is more he got his wicket, and was on to it at once. 'He's caught and bowled by Shastri!' he shouted, raising his two arms above his head as footballers do when they score a goal. Jim helped him out with the scoreboard which he found difficult to read, and gave his inter-over summaries with the same deep, authoritative voice that made him someone the listener could trust and believe. His judgments and arguments were as shrewd and knowledgeable as ever. It took us all back to the old days of *TMS*.

Listening to them in Alderney was their old colleague John Arlott, who had left the Test scene for ever at the end of the Centenary Test at Lord's in 1980. We spoke to him over the telephone and he assured us that he was sitting with a glass of claret in his hand (time 4.00 p.m.!). John emphasised that once he had retired, he never wanted to come to a Test match again. He never has, except for the first day of the First Test in the summer against Pakistan at Old Trafford. He had flown especially from Alderney to open the new Neville Cardus Suite in the new stand at the Warwick Road end. He stayed on the next day to watch some cricket, but of course it rained!

It was lovely to hear his soft Hampshire burr again, and it was good to hear him chuckle when we reminded him of his classic description of the streaker in 1975. I am sure that thousands of listeners appreciated hearing these three great commentators and lovers of cricket again. They certainly made our day.

Fourth Day

Henry Blofeld

In 1987, I made rather a habit of arriving at Lord's in the early morning with the milk bottles. It may have something to do with the fact that I live in London that I continually get landed with the *Today* programme, but it has its compensations, for at that time of the day one does not have to queue to get into the car park. Of course, Johnners lives just round the corner and Lord's is almost his back garden, but he has reached the stage in life where early morning starts like this are nothing more than distant memories. Or maybe he has forgotten how to set his alarm clock.

On the Sunday of the Bicentenary match I had driven down to Moreton-in-the-Marsh for the BBC to watch Gloucestershire put it across Nottinghamshire to the tune of two runs in the Sunday League, a defect which cost Nottinghamshire this particular title. Moreton has a lovely country ground from which you can see just one small house, and it is ringed by the most handsome trees. Gloucestershire first staged County Championship matches there in 1885, but after the 1889 season, W.G. Grace took first-class cricket away from Moreton because of the poor quality of the teas.

In 1987 teas were lavish in the extreme as I told listeners to Stuart Hall's *Sunday Sport* show, and they will even have put Nancy, who presides over the Players' and Committee Dining-rooms at Lord's and is out on her own, on her toes.

On Monday, then, after parking my car at the Nursery End – as usual it had taken a while to persuade the cark park attendants that I was still on urgent business, for they can be a suspicious lot – I climbed the pavilion stairs to Nancy's kitchen for a cup of tea. I revealed to Radio 4 listeners that the weather was good and that I had seen a tray of cold roast chickens being carried into one of the hospitality tents at the Nursery end and then I returned to Nancy who, for the second time in the summer, produced a scrummy plate of scrambled eggs which set me up for the day. Then it was back to business. The *TMS* team were all in good time – yes, even C.M-J. (The following morning when there was no play I am ashamed to say that I was the one with the red face using the traffic jams as an excuse.)

Once again we had a stream of important visitors to the box and I was in the middle of my first 20-minute spell of commentary when Peter Baxter whispered 'Marshall' in my ear just as fine leg, who was down below us and out of our sight, and who I imagined was Courtney Walsh, had fielded a ball. As he spoke I thought Peter was pointing to fine leg. I didn't know what had got into our producer, for the MCC side was batting and Marshall was playing for the MCC. I stood up and leaned out of the window and sure enough Walsh was the fielder at fine leg. It confirmed my impression that our producer had finally gone barmy. But when I sat down again I looked to my left and sitting on the other side of The Bearded Wonder was none other than Malcolm Marshall. So maybe it is not straitjacket time quite yet for poor old Backers.

Marshall told me how important it was for him to do well in this match with the eyes of the cricket-playing world focussed on Lord's. This was a sentiment expressed most strongly by all the participants who visited the box. It was responsible, too, for producing an old-fashioned game of cricket with contestants playing at their very best, determined to produce only their best and the motivation was simply the joy of taking part. The central figure on this Monday was Gordon Greenidge, who battled his way to a hundred with extraordinary determination. It is always a joy to describe an innings by Greenidge, although this one was a little slow by his usual standards. He left no one in any doubt about what a considerable batsman he is. Graham Gooch emphasised the form he had found in the first innings with an innings of 70, which was a more confident knock than his 117 in the first. The Boil was in ecstasy. The others all gave us glimpses of their exciting powers, and they made commentary easy.

I had the luck to be on the air when Graeme Pollock and Mike Procter paid a visit to the box. It was a great sadness that the selectors for this match had not asked Pollock to play. He had only just retired and was one of the great players of this or any other generation and surely deserved a place. Another surprising omission had been Graeme Hick. Our two South African visitors laughed and reminisced their way through several moments in their careers. Pollock is very modest, but he reluctantly admitted that perhaps the best Test innings he had played had been against England at Trent Bridge in 1965 when he slaughtered Tom Cartwright, at the time the most economical bowler in the world. It was a great match for the Pollocks, for Graeme's brother, Peter, took five wickets in each England innings.

During the lunch interval The Boil and I hosted the call-the-commentators half-hour and dealt, I hope with verve and excitement, with the usual splendid array of questions. The saddest moment of another truly memorable day came right at the end after Mike Gatting's declaration. After his 188 in the first innings, Sunil Gavaskar was, in his last innings at Lord's, reminded of what a great leveller cricket can be. His off-stump was uprooted in gloomy light by Marshall in the first over of the innings. He returned to the Lord's pavilion for the last time, to another standing ovation, but this time with nought and not 188 against his name. A great cricketer disappeared into history. And of course, almost as important, *TMS* had been given four cakes and three bottles of Champagne during the day and by the end not much was left of any of them.

Fifth Day

Trevor Bailey

The Day That The Rains Came Down

One of the great attractions of cricket is its unpredictability, which makes fore-casting such a tricky business. However, few predictions can have turned out to be as wrong as the one I made as early as the first day of the MCC Bicentenary match, and repeated during the next three. I said that the greatest excitement would occur on the final day of what proved a delightfully entertaining match. In my defence I must say that I still think it would have been, if the heavens had not opened.

Tuesday's one redeeming feature was that the rain was so heavy that the outfield resembled a lake and the umpires were able to call it off early so that there was not much hanging around. The *TMS* team did their best to satisfy the legion of listeners who prefer us when it rains. The batting, bowling and fielding awards were to be made before lunch by Sir 'Gubby' Allen and Denis Compton. At the appointed time the latter was found to be missing and none of us were even vaguely surprised, as over the years Denis has acquired a reputation for being slightly unreliable, something which he himself has never been able to understand. However, on this occasion the great man was for once completely blameless, as he was a victim of a five-mile hold-up on the motorway following a multiple crash. What I should have liked to have heard was his conversation with a well-intentioned policeman who refused to allow an understandably harassed, frustrated and late Compton to take his car into Lord's.

Quite logically the batting award went to Sunil Gavaskar. His was not only a beautifully executed innings, but also provided a most appropriate setting for the 'little master' to end his first-class career. Malcolm Marshall won the bowling award and on a 'featherbed' was still able to demonstrate why he was currently the best fast bowler in the world. Although Clive Rice brought off two brilliant catches and fielded very well, I was still somewhat surprised that he was adjudged the best fieldsman ahead of Roger Harper. Roger's run-out of Graham Gooch was easily the most spectacular piece of fielding I saw all summer. In addition, he made a difficult catch look ridiculously easy, while his speed and agility enabled him to cover as much ground as any two normal fielders.

Haynes gives Roger Harper the 'high five' after Harper's remarkable run-out of Gooch at Lord's. Dujon and Gavaskar are in the background.   Patrick Eagar

MCC 1ST INNINGS v REST OF THE WORLD (LORD'S BICENTENARY MATCH) ON 20,21,22,24,26 AUGUST, 1987

IN	OUT	MINS	No.	BATSMAN	HOW OUT	BOWLER	RUNS	WKT	TOTAL	6s	4s	BALLS	NOTES ON DISMISSAL TOSS: MCC
11·02	1·48	124	1	C.G. GREENIDGE	C' HARPER	QADIR	52	2	96	·	9	94	Lofted on drive - perfectly judged high catch by tall dp mid-on
11·02	11·21	19	2	B.C. BROAD	LBW	IMRAN	10	1	21	·	2	14	Played no stroke to ball that 'straightened'.
11·23	5·14	287	3	G.A. GOOCH	RUN OUT (HARPER)		117	4	254	·	18	211	(60' F.C. Superb stop and direct hit by bowler.
1·50	3·01	71	4	D.I. GOWER	C' DUJON	HARPER	8	3	151	·	·	54	Defensive edge to leg-break (to him) - Harper's 2nd ball.
3·03	2·04	314	5	M.W. GATTING *	BOWLED	WALSH	179	5	455	·	26	272	Missed cut - ball clipped off stump and removed leg bail.
5·16	2·04	202	6	C.E.B. RICE	NOT OUT		59			·	8	157	
			7	R.J. SHASTRI									
			8	R.J. HADLEE									
			9	M.D. MARSHALL	} DID NOT BAT								
			10	J.E. EMBUREY									
			11	B.N. FRENCH †									

* CAPTAIN † WICKET-KEEPER **EXTRAS** b 11 lb 15 w 1 nb 3 = **30** 0' 63' 802 balls (inc 3 no balls)

UMPIRES: H.D. BIRD & D.R. SHEPHERD **TOTAL** (133·1 OVERS - 513 MINUTES) **455·5 DECLARED** at 2·04pm on 2nd day.

15 OVERS 3 BALLS/HOUR
3·41 RUNS/OVER
56 RUNS/100 BALLS

BOWLER	O	M	R	W		HRS	OVERS	RUNS
IMRAN	25	6	97	1	·	1	14	51
WALSH	28·1	6	102	1	·	2	15	45
KAPIL DEV	24	8	54	0	√	3	16	40
ABDUL QADIR	16·2	7	30	1	·	4	16	46
HARPER	34	5	125	1	·	5	15	60
MIANDAD	5·4	0	21	0	#	6	17	38
			26	1		7	14	68
	133·1	32	455	5		8	16	67

2ND NEW BALL taken at 11·10am 2nd day
- MCC 302·4 after 97·4 overs

RUNS	MINS	OVERS	LAST 50 (no.of balls)
50	50	11·4	50
100	135	32·3	85
150	197	47·1	62
200	258	65·4	61
250	308	78·0	50
300	378	97·2	70
350	423	107·5	45
400	472	120·1	49
450	507	131·4	35

LUNCH: 96-1 [39 OVERS / 113 MIN] GREENIDGE 52' (94) GOOCH 27' (97)
TEA: 177-3 [60 OVERS / 238 MIN] GOOCH 89' (216) GATTING 6' (29)
STUMPS: 291-4 (1ST DAY) [96 OVERS / 371 MIN] GATTING 68' (172) RICE 14' (60)
LUNCH: 427-4 [127 OVERS / 490 MIN] GATTING 158' (251) RICE 56' (179)

WKT	PARTNERSHIP		RUNS	MINS
1st	Greenidge	Broad	21	19
2nd	Greenidge	Gooch	75	102
3rd	Gooch	Gower	55	71
4th	Gooch	Gatting	103	110
5th	Gatting	Rice	201	202
			455	

COMPILED by BILL FRINDALL

REST OF THE WORLD 1ST INNINGS

IN	OUT	MINS	No.	BATSMAN	HOW OUT	BOWLER	RUNS	WKT	TOTAL	6s	4s	BALLS	NOTES ON DISMISSAL
2·16	3·34	404	1	S.M. GAVASKAR	C' AND BOWLED	SHASTRI	188	7	389	·	23	351	FIRST HUNDRED AT LORD'S IN FINAL FIRST-CLASS MATCH. Mistimed drive
2·16	3·14	58	2	D.L. HAYNES	C' RICE	MARSHALL	23	1	46	·	3	49	Edged drive at widish ball low to 1st slip.
3·16	4·41	63	3	D.B. VENGSARKAR	C' GOOCH	MARSHALL	22	2	93	·	4	49	Fended short ball from round wicket low to 2nd gully.
4·43	5·33	50	4	A.R. BORDER *	C' RICE	SHASTRI	26	3	148	1	3	39	Mistimed off drive - diving 2-handed catch at wide mid-off.
5·35	11·35	28	5	P.J.L. DUJON †	C' GOOCH	MARSHALL	9	4	173	·	1	31	Edged drive to 3rd slip.
11·37	2·58	159	6	IMRAN KHAN	BOWLED	SHASTRI	82	5	353	2	10	145	Played on - underedged backfoot offside force.
3·00	3·19	19	7	KAPIL DEV	C' MARSHALL	EMBUREY	13	6	372	·	2	25	Skier to long-off - ran in.
3·21	(6·00)	31	8	R.A. HARPER	NOT OUT		17			·	2	42	
3·36	(6·00)	16	9	C.A. WALSH	NOT OUT		21			1	2	19	
			10	JAVED MIANDAD	} DID NOT BAT								
			11	ABDUL QADIR									

* CAPTAIN † WICKET-KEEPER **EXTRAS** b 3 lb 8 w 4 nb 5 = **20** 4' 56' 750 balls (inc 6 no-balls)

TOTAL (124 OVERS - 423 MINUTES) **421·7 DECLARED** (at stumps on 3rd day)

17 OVERS 3 BALLS/HOUR
3·39 RUNS/OVER
56 RUNS/100 BALLS

BOWLER	O	M	R	W		HRS	OVERS	RUNS
MARSHALL	20	3	53	3	#	1	15	46
HADLEE	21	2	71	0	·	2	18	47
RICE	12	1	63	0	·	3	16	55
SHASTRI	42	4	130	3	#/·	4	17	54
EMBUREY	29	7	93	1	·	5	21	75
			11			6	14	61
	124	17	421	7		7	22	76

2ND NEW BALL taken at 1·44pm 3rd day
- REST 264·4 after 85·2 overs

RUNS	MINS	OVERS	LAST 50 (no.of balls)
50	64	16·2	64
100	128	34·5	64
150	181	49·3	53
200	232	63·4	51
250	280	79·5	48
300	326	93·1	46
350	368	104·4	42
400	413	120·3	45

TEA: 69-1 [21 OVERS / 84 MIN] GAVASKAR 31' (86) VENGSARKAR 8' (14)
STUMPS: 169-3 (2ND DAY) [57 OVERS / 202 MIN] GAVASKAR 80' (201) DUJON 8' (25)
LUNCH: 264-4 [85 OVERS / 293 MIN] GAVASKAR 128' (293) IMRAN 43' (64)
TEA: 391-7 [119 OVERS / 410 MIN] HARPER 8' (19) WALSH 0' (4)
START DELAYED UNTIL 5·48pm (RAIN AT TEA)
STUMPS: 421-7 (3RD DAY) [124 OVERS / 423 MIN] HARPER 17' (31) WALSH 21' (16)

WKT	PARTNERSHIP		RUNS	MINS
1st	Gavaskar	Haynes	46	58
2nd	Gavaskar	Vengsarkar	47	63
3rd	Gavaskar	Border	55	50
4th	Gavaskar	Dujon	25	28
5th	Gavaskar	Imran	180	159
6th	Gavaskar	Kapil Dev	19	19
7th	Gavaskar	Harper	17	13
8th	Harper	Walsh	32'	16
			421	

COMPILED by BILL FRINDALL

M.C.C. 2ND INNINGS (34 RUNS AHEAD ON FIRST INNINGS)

IN	OUT	MINS	No	BATSMAN	HOW OUT	BOWLER	RUNS	WKT	TOTAL	6s	4s	BALLS	NOTES ON DISMISSAL
11.00	5.02	301	1	C.G. GREENIDGE	BOWLED	QADIR	122	4	289	2	12	223	Down wicket - missed leg-break. 26 of 10 reverse sweeps
11.00	11.24	24	2	B.C. BROAD	C† DUJON	KAPIL DEV	2	1	11	·	·	7	Edged push at midwith offside ball.
11.26	2.18	132	3	G.A. GOOCH	BOWLED	HARPER	70	2	146	·	12	117	Missed off-break.
2.20	4.14	93	4	D.I. GOWER	C† BORDER	IMRAN	40	3	231	·	7	74	Edged outswinger (to him) to slip.
4.16	5.08	52	5	R.J. HADLEE	C† IMRAN	WALSH	36	5	293	·	6†	39	† plus one five · Lofted on-drive - mid-on at 3rd attempt - high catch
5.04	(5.50)	46	6	R.J. SHASTRI	NOT OUT		10	·	·	·	1	38	
5.10	5.33	23	7	J.E. EMBUREY	C† HAYNES	QADIR	7	6	308	·	1	14	Well-judged skier at long-off
5.35	(5.50)	15	8	C.E.B. RICE	NOT OUT		4	·	·	·	·	17	
			9	M.W. GATTING *									
			10	M.D. MARSHALL									
			11	B.N. FRENCH †									

*CAPTAIN †WICKET-KEEPER

EXTRAS b 16 lb 10 w - nb 1 = 27   2s 39† 529 balls (inc. 1 no-ball)

TOTAL (88 OVERS - 349 MINUTES) 318-6 DECLARED at 5.50 pm on 4th DAY

15 OVERS 0 BALLS/HOUR
3.61 RUNS/OVER
60 RUNS/100 BALLS

BOWLER	O	M	R	W	nb		HRS	OVERS	RUNS
IMRAN	13	3	83	1	·	1	14	38	
KAPIL DEV	7	0	21	1	·	2	16	66	
WALSH	12	3	54	1	·	3	17	50	
ABDUL QADIR	36	9	112	2	·	4	15	58	
HARPER	20	2	72	1	·	5	14	77	
					26				
	88	18	318	6					

	RUNS	MINS	OVERS	LAST 50 (in mins)
50	72	16.0	72
100	114	28.5	42
150	165	43.4	51
200	217	56.4	52
250	280	71.5	63
300	327	81.0	47

LUNCH: 104-1 (132 AHEAD) 30 OVERS 120 MIN GREENIDGE 31* (4s) GOOCH 60 (94)

TEA: 212-2 62 OVERS 240 MIN GREENIDGE 90* (3s) GOWER 23* (30)

REST OF THE WORLD SET 353

WKT	PARTNERSHIP		RUNS	MINS
1st	Greenidge	Broad	11	24
2nd	Greenidge	Gooch	135	132
3rd	Greenidge	Gower	85	93
4th	Greenidge	Hadlee	58	46
5th	Hadlee	Shastri	4	4
6th	Shastri	Emburey	15	23
7th	Shastri	Rice	10*	15
			318	

COMPILED by BILL FRINDALL

REST OF THE WORLD 2ND INNINGS NEEDING 353 RUNS TO WIN

IN	OUT	MINS	No	BATSMAN	HOW OUT	BOWLER	RUNS	WKT	TOTAL	6s	4s	BALLS	NOTES ON DISMISSAL
6.02	6.04	2	1	S.M. GAVASKAR	BOWLED	MARSHALL	0	1	2	·	·	3	Off stump out - break-back through 'gate'
6.02	(6.22)	20	2	D.L. HAYNES	NOT OUT		3			·	·	8	
6.06	(6.22)	16	3	R.A. HARPER	NOT OUT		9			·	1	16	
			4										
			5										
			6										
			7										
			8										
			9										
			10										
			11										

*CAPTAIN †WICKET-KEEPER

EXTRAS b - lb 1 w - nb - = 1   0s 1† 27 balls

TOTAL (4.3 OVERS - 20 MINUTES) 13-1

13 OVERS 3 BALLS/HOUR
2.88 RUNS/OVER
48 RUNS/100 BALLS

BOWLER	O	M	R	W
MARSHALL	2.3	0	10	1
HADLEE	2	1	2	0
			1	
	4.3	1	13	1

STUMPS: 13-1 (4.3 OVERS; 20 MIN) HAYNES 3* (2s) (4th DAY) NEEDING 340 HARPER 9* (4s)

RAIN PREVENTED PLAY ON FIFTH DAY

MATCH DRAWN

AWARDS: BATTING - S.M. GAVASKAR
BOWLING - M.D. MARSHALL
FIELDING - C.E.B. RICE

ADJUDICATORS: SIR GEORGE ALLEN
D.C.S. COMPTON

WKT	PARTNERSHIP		RUNS	MINS
1st	Gavaskar	Haynes	2	2
2nd	Haynes	Harper	11*	16
			13	

COMPILED by BILL FRINDALL

Views from the Boundary

Brian Johnston

We had a varied selection of guests on our Saturday lunchtime spot this summer. We started at Old Trafford with Professor Sir Bernard Lovell, famous astronomer and cricket-lover. He was educated in Bristol and played cricket for Bristol University. He saw Hammond's first match for Gloucestershire and was also present at Taunton when Jack Hobbs scored his 125th century. When he joined the staff of Manchester University in 1936 he used to pay sixpence to watch Lancashire, and seems to have been greatly impressed by Cyril Washbrook's fielding at cover. He is now a vice-president of the club and persuaded them to put his two light meters on the Wilson Stand. These are like a clock face, and when the hands point to 12.15 the light is perfect. At 12.00 it is bad. They could be adjusted to fit the different backgrounds of all the Test venues, and cost something between £1,000 and £2,000.

A year ago he was asked by TCCB to design some electronic aids for umpires, to help with lbw decisions, run-outs and catches behind the wicket. With two very sensitive cameras at each end of the ground he has devised a system which will tell the umpires (by means of a buzzer in the ear, or a light flashing on the scoreboard) whether the ball would have gone on to hit the stumps *after* hitting the batsman's pads. The same cameras could also decide on run-outs by relating the time the ball hit the stumps to when the bat first touched the popping crease. To detect whether the ball has hit the bat or pad when there is an appeal for caught behind, Sir Bernard has tried inserting a minute gadget into the handle of the bat. He tried it out at the beginning of the season, but unfortunately the gadget, which is super-sensitive and fragile, disintegrated the first time the bat hit the ball hard.

However, he is certain that all these three 'aids' would help the umpires without taking away their responsibility for making the final decision. The one snag appears to be the cost, possibly up to £200,000 for the four cameras and their installation. But they could be transferred from ground to ground.

Sir Bernard has led an exciting life at Jodrell Bank. His greatest achievement was when his giant telescope detected the first sputnik in 1957, and his ambition is to put a large radio telescope into space with radio links back to earth. It is not surprising therefore that he finds modern cricket dull compared with the greats whom he saw as a boy. And by the way, he confirmed what Patrick Moore told us two years ago that the surface of the moon would be far too dusty to play cricket on.

At Lord's our guest was a famous actor who has made more films (142) than any other British actor. He has been described as tall, dark and gruesome, and is

Someone who takes a view far beyond any boundary – Sir Bernard Lovell.

Rex Features

perhaps unfairly connected with horror films. True enough, he made 15 of them, playing Dracula six times, and also the 'creature' in *The Curse of Frankenstein*. They were tough to make. His face and head were often swathed in bandages which made it difficult for him to eat his lunch. And he has lost count of the number of times he was speared through the eyes and heart.

Christopher Lee was certainly tall (six foot four) and dark but far from gruesome when he joined us in the box. I was surprised at his knowledge of cricket and at his tremendous enthusiasm for the game. As a boy he had an action like Mike Procter or Max Walker and was a fastish bowler, bringing the ball down from his considerable height. He played for his school, Wellington, and while there was lucky to see Jack Hobbs in a match for Surrey against Oxford University, and remembers Bradman for his fierce pull shot from outside the off-stump. He knew Bev Lyon, the Gloucestershire captain, and through him met Wally Hammond. He said that if you look at the old scorecards you will often see c Lyon b Pasher. But Lyon told him that Hammond used to make many of their catches, and flip the ball quickly to Lyon at second slip so that he was credited with the catch.

Christopher was with 260 Squadron Desert Air Force, and once during a spell off from fighting took nine wickets on matting. After the War he played for a side called the Bowler Hat Club organised by Trevor Howard. The first ball he bowled for the side was declared 'dead'. He did not let go of it until his arm had completed its full circle, and the ball shot backwards to the boundary behind the bowler's end. He knew all the Hollywood actors who played for C. Aubrey Smith's side at Griffith Park: Nigel (Willie) Bruce, David Niven, Errol Flynn and, of course, Boris Karloff, whose real name was William Henry Pratt. Karloff always came to Lord's and The Oval where he was a member and, like Trevor Howard and Aubrey Smith, always had a clause in his film contracts stipulating no filming during a Lord's Test. Aubrey

Smith ('Round the Corner' because of his action) was an absolute dictator on the field and deplored any slackness. His house, 'Cold Water Canyon' had a replica of Old Father Time and the MCC flag flying from the flagpole.

Christopher is a member of MCC and comes to Lord's whenever he can. He dislikes action replays which question the umpire's decision, and he hates the intimidatory tactics of the modern fast bowlers. He still thinks that Larwood was the fastest bowler he ever saw, and that 'Toey' Tayfield was the best off-spinner. I suspect he likes golf as much as cricket. He used to be a scratch golfer, once playing in the Amateur Championship, and has played in the USA in pro-am tournaments with all the great names of golf, except one: Ben Hogan. He evidently only plays privately with close friends.

I ended our conversation by asking him who was the most attractive actress he ever bit in the neck. He had bitten so many that he found it difficult to choose, but he did say that the greatest actress with whom he played was Bette Davis.

Our guest at Headingley was Michael Parkinson, whose father desperately wanted him to play for Yorkshire. He did everything he could to achieve this. He gave Parky his first bat when Parky was four, and took him to watch his first county cricket at Bramall Lane a year later. Parky himself was to become a professional and was good enough to go to the Yorkshire nets under 'Ticker' Mitchell and Maurice Leyland. But he was just not good enough, although some of his companions at the nets such as Close and Illingworth went on to captain England.

Parky used to go in first for Barnsley with Dickie Bird and once against Harrogate they put on 210. Parky got a hundred but ran out Dickie when he was 98. This was hard luck on Dickie, as he previously made four ducks in a row, three of them first balls. Dickie was so nervous that he chewed through the fingers of his batting gloves.

After the War at about the time of Suez Parky actually played for Hampshire club and ground but then as captain he was whisked off as an intelligence officer to the canal zone. Just as well, perhaps: his father would never have approved had he opted to play for Hampshire.

Parky became a journalist and wrote about sport and the cinema, and would dearly have liked to have been a cricket reporter. He was also tried as a TV commentator but after his trial gave himself minus two marks out of ten. He used to run an All Stars Cricket XI, one of whose members was the Alderman, Don Mosey. Parky said Don played hard to win. He was a brisk, military medium and was a real competitor, and also a particularly loud appealer. But Parky said that Don always accepted the umpire's decision, and only swore at him after he had passed him!

Parky is unashamedly a hero-worshipper, which is why he enjoyed his chat show so much, meeting so many famous people whom he had worshipped from afar – except of course that dreaded Emu. His greatest hero was Len Hutton, the 'benchmark' of all opening batsmen. He told a lovely story about Len when he was a selector. He had been silent for a long time while discussions went on about the capabilities of various players. After a while the chairman, Alec Bedser, asked him to say something. 'Did you ever see Ginger Rogers and Fred Astaire dance?' was

Len's contribution! Parky's best ever footballer was George Best – 'the pleasantest rogue' he knew – who had a compelling personality which made him stand out in a crowded room. But when Parky went to visit him in prison, he was upset to find he could not pick out George at all from the other prisoners in their grey prison clothes.

Parky is a regular visitor to Australia where he has a delightful flat overlooking Elizabeth Bay. He feels that there is a North Country affinity with the Australians, with whom he himself gets on very well.

And, of course, he had to mention another Yorkshireman whom he interviewed on his chat show, and has written about many times – Geoff Boycott. Parky first saw him when Geoff was aged 15 and wearing National Health specs, and admires his tremendous dedication and application: if his life depended on someone making runs he would pick Geoff every time. He feels that David Bairstow was right when he said of Boycott: 'Stop looking at his bad points and learn from his good ones'.

Parky plays a big part in helping to run Berkshire schools cricket, and in his spare time plays golf, often with his wife Mary who he says is twice as good as he is.

At Edgbaston for the first time in 'A View from the Boundary' we entertained a king in the box. King John of Wales – Barry John. He was given this title by a doting Welsh public, who thought him the greatest ever fly-half rugby had known. But although he says that boys in Wales only play cricket to keep fit for rugby, he has himself aways played and followed the game, especially the fortunes of Glamorgan.

I put my foot in it early on. He said how much he admired Tony Lewis and his championship-winning side of 1969. So I asked him what he thought of the 1948 team which won the championship under Wilf Wooller. 'I never really saw them so I cannot give an opinion. You see, I was only aged three at the time.' (Collapse of stout commentator.) Barry used to play for Cowbridge and was a third change bowler and a six or seven batsman. He qualified early in his career for membership of the Primary Club in a game against Llangarren, and once took three wickets in one over when playing for Tony Lewis.

But, of course, his skills were at rugby football: 25 caps for Wales at fly-half, a record 180 points on the British Lions tour of 1971 and an early retirement at the age of 27. His unbounded hero was Gareth Edwards, who was his partner in all but two of his internationals. Barry was called an elusive creature because he was so difficult to lay a hand on. He would glide and side-step through the opposition. I asked him his secret. 'I saw things early', he said. He had an unusual way of passing, running towards his centre with the ball, unless he spotted an opening, which he would then dart through. He escaped serious injury in spite of being the target of the wing forwards, partly because of his elusiveness but also because he was remarkably strong.

Barry became a great place-kicker and was one of the first to employ the 'round the corner' approach to the ball. If you ever see a film of him taking a place-kick, watch how he always takes out his gumshield first and hands it to Gareth for safe-keeping.

In his No 10 jersey he was the orchestrator of the threequarters and he left the game in triumph. He had announced that he would score a try in the final minute of his last game – and he did.

It was lovely to meet this mythical king. He played down his skills, was amusing and admitted that he grew three feet taller every time he walked out on to Cardiff Arms Park. My last question to him was about cricket. I compared the hugging and kissing that goes on in Test matches when someone makes a catch or takes a wicket with what happens in rugby. No matter how brilliant the try or the kick, no one ever pats the scorer on the back nor shakes his hand. So how would he feel about being kissed and hugged if he were to take a wicket at cricket? 'I would bowl a wide in order to avoid it', he replied.

Scccchhhh . . . you know who? Yes, quite right. William Franklyn was our guest at The Oval. And incidentally he didn't make the 'Scccchhhh' noise in that famous television advertisement which ran for something like 15 years. A lot of people think that Bill is an Australian. But in fact he was taken Down Under as a young boy in 1926 by his father, Leo, who went for 18 months to play in musical comedies and stayed for ten years. Leo was not only a very fine comedian – many of you will have seen him in the Brian Rix farces – but he was mad on cricket and got to know all the great Australian cricketers of that era. Bill showed me a photograph of himself as a small boy with a bat on which were the autographs of the 1924 and 1928 Australian teams. Leo used to lead a team of actors against Australian Test cricketers, and once caught and bowled Don Bradman.

Bill was educated at Haileybury in Melbourne and was coached there and played for Under-11 and -13 teams. He used to bowl leg-breaks and remembers Arthur Mailey coming to their home and demonstrating how to bowl a googly in the sitting-room with a teacup as the ball. His first visual memory of first-class cricket was in 1932, when he and his father stood on the hill at Sydney and saw Stan McCabe make his famous 187 not out against the bodyline bowling of Larwood and Voce. When they returned to England he saw every day of the 1938 Oval Test and of course especially remembers Len Hutton's 344.

He has played all types of cricket in England. He once played for the Stage against the Cross Arrows and had the honour of being bowled out by one of Jim Swanton's 'holy rollers'. Ray Smith of Essex also arranged for him to have a 'trial' for an Essex side against Slough. To his surprise he took four wickets cheaply for only nine runs. Feeling rather superior and sorry for the opposition he said to Ray Smith, 'Do you think I ought to ease up a bit?' 'No', replied Ray, who knew that the next batsman was a big hitter, and thought that Bill needed taking down a peg, 'Just carry on as you are.' Result – Bill finished with an analysis of 4 for 84, and learned a lesson. As Fred Trueman would say: 'Cricket is a funny game'.

Bill still runs a team called The Sargent Men who play in aid of the Malcolm Sargent Cancer Fund for children. The late Leonard Rossiter was a good all-rounder and once had a trial for Lancashire. Ian Lavender keeps wicket and Francis Matthews also 'turns out'.

Our guest in his native Yorkshire, Michael Parkinson. Rex Features

William Franklyn, our guest at The Oval. Rex Features

Barry John slips away again – but we tackled him at Edgbaston. Colorsport

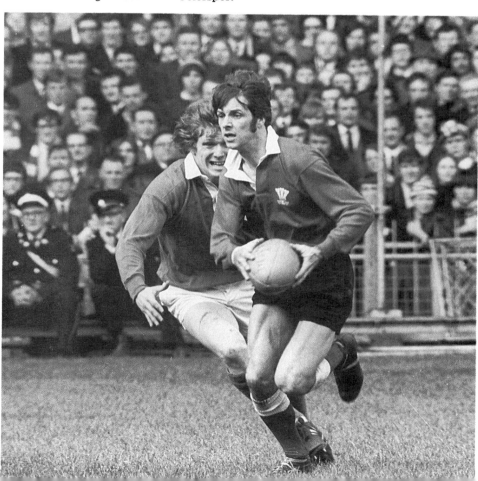

As one who had been in Australia during Jardine's tour in 1932, I asked him what he thought of the bodyline film. He didn't enjoy it much, especially when a fielder made a catch at square-leg and then appealed, and also when the wicketkeeper was shown standing up to Larwood! One thing he didn't know was that Lord Harris, the villain of the piece in the film, had died six months before the tour started.

Bill spends his time between television and the stage, and basically prefers the latter. In the summer it gives him more time to watch cricket during the week and to play on Sundays. In the winter he can spend his mornings having a net. Bill told us how much he owed to his father. Leo had a love of cricket and also had the actor's priceless gift of 'timing'. He passed both these on to Bill, who summed up for me his attitude to cricket: 'I'm addicted', he said.

For the Bicentenary match at Lord's we were especially honoured to have as a guest His Royal Highness the Duke of Edinburgh. Because he was due to be at Balmoral at the time of the match, I went to talk to him in his study at Buckingham Palace to record the interview beforehand.

He was especially modest about his own cricket skills: 'I was never very good'. He started at his preparatory school at Cheam where he was described as 'an energetic all-rounder, highly unsympathetic to stone-walling'. When he went to Gordonstoun he became captain of the cricket XI and was an off-break bowler. Later, when in the Navy, he played in Malta and at a place called Akaba, which he found too hot for cricket. After the War, as President of the National Playing Fields Association, he played in a number of charity matches and there are several photographs of him bowling in dark glasses. He took 1 for 12 against Hampshire at Bournemouth, 'the best cricket ground I have ever played on'. On Lord Porchester's ground at Highdene he once made 25 and saw New Zealander John Reid score what was said to be the fastest fifty ever scored in any class of cricket. But his greatest triumph was when he got Tom Graveney caught at short-leg in a match at Arundel.

As a boy the Duke was taken to Lord's to watch cricket and the names he best remembered were Bradman, Hammond and Duckworth. He said that the Prince of Wales, the Duke of York and Prince Edward played cricket in the ordinary course of events at school, but that he did not have them especially coached.

When the Lord's Taverners were founded in 1950 he was asked by the founder, Martin Boddey, to be their first president. But he suggested that he should be given the title of 12th Man, and he has been Patron and 12th Man ever since. He helped with suggestions for some of the 'games' at the annual Lord's Taverners' Ball. He thought that the normal charity ball was a bit of a bore, so suggested that something different should take place – hence the annual sporting event which was the main feature of the Ball for many years. There was a cricket match, an athletics meeting and a rowing race to name but a few, and the Lord's Taverners always had to win. Prince Philip was present at the athletics meeting. I remember it only too well: I dislocated my shoulder during a three-legged race in which I was the middle man between Macdonald Hobley and Peter Haigh. We slipped up and I could not break my fall as my arms were around their necks! Prince Philip also started the boat race with the

Our Royal guest for the MCC Bicentenary match, but happier with four-in-hand, HRH the Duke of Edinburgh.   Popperfoto

immortal words, 'Are you ready Oxford and Cambridge? Are you sober Lord's Taverners?'.

He said how pleased he was to be asked to be president of MCC in 1949. He found the reputedly stuffy members of the Committee 'a jolly lot' and in his speech at the annual dinner he said that he felt he was the link between the first family and the first sport. It was nice to hear that he felt that cricket was the first sport, not soccer!

In 1974 the Duke became president for the second time and I suggested that he was the only person ever to have been president twice. But he corrected me; he had been told that there had been one or possibly two others, although he could not remember who. I have checked with MCC since then, and Prince Philip was quite right. In 1853 The Marquess of Worcester was president, and became so again in 1877, when he had become the Eighth Duke of Beaufort. And in 1837 Viscount Grimston likewise was president and took office a second time as Second Earl of Verulam in 1867.

I asked Prince Philip why he had accepted a second time and he jokingly replied that 'it would be quite amusing to have in the record books'. But he later realised why he had been asked: in 1974 MCC were putting up the subscriptions and they must have thought that he was the best person to sell the idea at the Annual General Meeting! I asked him if he liked the New Mound Stand which he had opened on 4 May. 'I didn't open it, I launched it', he replied. 'I thought it would sail.'

He had some more serious things to say about sport for the young. There is a severe shortage of playing fields due to the incursion of developers building on playing fields sold by local councils. He is all for team games and competitive sport, even though many teachers today seem to be against them. He believes games like cricket teach young people how to win and lose, and how to get on in society, and feels that sport and games are part of social education.

I ended by asking him whether there was anything that he would like to change in first-class cricket. He said that he disliked all the hugging and embracing which went on, and that he wished the players' trousers would fit better!

The World Cup
England and Group B

Christopher Martin—Jenkins, Peter Baxter

Monday 28 September, London Less than a fortnight after the last ball of the 1987 English season had been bowled the England team were assembling at Heathrow Airport and with them a party of journalists which included myself. I found myself recalling a remark someone made a few days ago when asking about my job: 'Ah, but you can't do that all the year round', he said.

There were the usual comments about tour haircuts. My own barber had apparently regarded the prospect of three months away as a challenge. He seemed to have made sure that no Pakistani barber would need to draw scissors on my account and left me with the comment 'That should keep you cool!'

Boarding the aeroplane to take us to Delhi marked the start of putting to the test the months of planning which have gone before. Suddenly the line on the bottom of so many telexes – 'See you in Delhi 29 September' – is becoming real. So farewell to two surprised infants and long-suffering wife and away to the mysteries of the east.

P.B.

England's squad for the 1987 World Cup.
Graham Morris

Tuesday 29 September, Delhi Arriving in Delhi after a sleepless overnight flight the last thing one would choose would be a day of two functions either side of wrestling with accreditation bureaucracy, but the evening reception for all the players taking part in the World Cup was a glittering occasion and a rare one, too, and I felt privileged to be there to witness the mingling of cricketers from all round the world. It was an appropriate launch to this so-called cricket extravaganza.

P.B.

Wednesday 30 September, Delhi After a morning in which I visited All India Radio to check that all my commentary facilities were in order it was time to go to the grand Nehru Stadium for the opening ceremony and inaugural match between India and Pakistan. By this time I had had plenty of opportunity to reacquaint myself with the system of Indian driving – biggest goes first – which works as long as an auto-rickshaw driver does not feel that his standing has been raised by the presence in his vehicle of an English journalist, a fact which may not be obvious to the driver of an inter-state lorry about to wipe him off the road.

The opening ceremony was a delightfully chaotic affair surrounded by the most rigorous security. One Indian television commentator was refused entry because he was 'armed' with throat lozenges and binoculars. The reason for the clamp-down was the presence of Prime Minister Rajiv Gandhi, who greeted the teams as they filed up to meet him in the stand. Then, as the umpires took the field, hundreds of balloons were released. It would be fairer to say that they had to be evicted because they seemed very reluctant to become airborne. One bunch did rise, only to become ensnared on a floodlight pylon. The rest slunk round the field and eventually had to be gathered by a bunch of pyjama-clad Keystone Cops to allow the game to start.

The game was played in its later stages under these magnificent floodlights and, for all that it was a festival occasion, was played with all the commitment you would expect from India and Pakistan. That night, against an Imran-less Pakistan, India showed themselves the more efficient unit in their 14-run victory.

P.B.

Thursday 1 October, Delhi Today the teams dispersed around the sub-continent for their final preparations with a week to the first game. England were Pakistan-bound on the same flight as the West Indies and Pakistan themselves, but we went on from our first arrival point in Rawalpindi. At least the players' bus turned right out of the airport to Rawalpindi and an hotel next to the 'Pindi cricket ground. The press bus, however, turned left to the modern capital, Islamabad, ten miles away, Pakistan's answer to Canberra with more than a touch of Milton Keynes about it.

P.B.

Monday 5 October, Rawalpindi A practice match had been arranged for England at the Rawalpindi club. It was something of a dress rehearsal for the press, too, on the ground where England and Pakistan will meet in a week's time. I used my time in Islamabad meeting the people at the Pakistan Broadcasting Corporation's head-quarters who would be arranging my facilities here.

At least I had a story to report when I got through to the *Today* programme from the ground. 'The good news,' I said, 'is that Gladstone Small has taken three wickets. The bad news is that they're three England wickets, because he's playing for the opposition in the practice.'

P.B.

Tuesday 6 October, Lahore We have now moved to Lahore where the press party has been more than doubled by a new influx from home. The BBC Radio contingent has been doubled by the arrival of Christopher Martin-Jenkins. We are quartered in the same hotel as the West Indies team, England's first opponents in the World Cup. The serious business is just around the corner.

P.B.

Tuesday 6 October, Lahore I write from a comfortable chair in my spacious and attractive room at the Pearl Continental Hotel, Lahore. Outside it is a hot, heavy day, but the air-conditioning in the hotel works well.

Lahore, at least near the hotel, is despite the heat and a dusty atmosphere, a city of parks and trees. This hotel has a handsome garden at the back with a pitch and putt golf course and a tennis court, the former sadly neglected. Only some of the English press group are staying here, the others being with the England team at the nearby Hilton Hotel.

After my adventurous journey out, which included a four-hour delay in Kuwait due to a bomb scare, I decided not to try to sleep in the middle of the day but to wait until the evening to try to get my body clock attuned to local time. Although feeling weary I took to the local golf club, the Gymkhana, with John Thicknesse and Jack Bannister and set off on a long course for a 12-hole match, accompanied by a platoon of caddies who eventually found even the wildest shots, emerging triumphantly from the jungle with the ball. When one drove into slight rough one found the ball sitting up nicely in a perfect lie every time! Perhaps as a result of this I ended up with the prize-money.

C.M-J.

Wednesday 7 October, Lahore Despite not having slept for 36 hours, I did not sleep all that well on Tuesday night but felt perfectly fit through this first full working day. England played quite a satisfactory warm-up match (although in this weather no one needs warming up) at the Gymkhana club, which used to be a Test ground and is set most picturesquely in a park with handsome broad-leafed trees all round. However, there was no telephone at the ground so in order to report the match I had to keep making sweaty 15-minute walks back to the hotel. Even there, communications were not straightforward. My first calls, at 6.00 a.m. BST and 7.25, got through on time but the BBC failed to contact me at 8.25 and there were various complications also in despatching my evening report. On one of my walks back I tried to take a short cut over the seven-foot fence bordering the park and ripped one of only two pairs of long trousers brought with me. I am hoping the hotel staff can patch it for me.

C.M-J.

Thursday 8 October, Lahore I had quite a good meal at the hotel restaurant with my two golfing colleagues plus Peter Baxter and John Woodcock. Today I watched the Pakistan versus Sri Lanka match on television and Peter and I did our best to report the match second-hand for various programmes on Radio 2 and Radio 4, although by no means all the calls got through.

C.M-J.

Thursday 8 October, Gujranwala Gujranwala, England's first venue, is some 40 miles north of Lahore and I resolved to go there to check out our commentary facilities at the ground. Micky Stewart, the cricket manager, offered me a seat in the car which was taking him there. We were able to chuckle together over such sub-continental delights as the haycart coming towards us down the outside lane of the dual carriageway. Not everything you see ahead of you on Pakistan's equivalent of the M1 is necessarily going in the same direction. On the way back we witnessed a spectacular crash as a tractor turned abruptly across the oncoming traffic and hit a small minibus which shot into the air and landed on its roof. The driver appeared to have been propelled out of his seat and landed on his feet, running. Five or six others tumbled from the wreckage but there seemed to be more wedged inside as our emotionless driver negotiated his way past the obstacle.

Gujranwala is a bustling, unlovely town, but the Municipal Stadium is magnificent. Micky was very impressed with the palatial dressing-rooms. I was slightly less so with the radio box. It certainly would not have been chosen by a broadcaster, as it has concrete blinkers which means that most of the occupants will have to look straight ahead and only the person in the front left-hand corner of the commentary box will be able to see the scoreboard. That will have to be the main commentator's seat.

After our inspection, Micky and I were taken to the home of the ground administrator for tea and a huge display of cakes and sandwiches was produced. In mid-morning it was rather overwhelming, but after so much effort we felt we must show willing. So we each selected a toasted sandwich and as Micky sank his teeth into the first mouthful our host said, 'I hope you like green chillies'. Micky's eyes were out on stalks but he carried on manfully.

We have seen enough of our journey to know that tomorrow morning's 6.00 a.m. departure from Lahore is indeed a necessity. A few hundred miles to the south in Hyderabad the World Cup is already underway as Pakistan overcome strong resistance from the Sri Lankan batsmen. Tomorrow will see England enter the fray.

We will be broadcasting the whole game from 5.00 a.m. at home with Tony Lewis, Jack Bannister, Mike Selvey and a new recruit in Peter Roebuck, all led by Christopher Martin-Jenkins.

P.B.

Friday 9 October, Gujranwala The match in Gujranwala was a long, exhausting but memorable day for all concerned. We set alarm clocks for 5.00 a.m. and left at six in a minibus convoy led by police, blue lights flashing, team next and press behind, some 30 of us.

The journey through the suburbs of Lahore was extraordinary. The streets were teeming with people, the road ahead and around us packed with bicycles, rickshaws, battered old Morris Minors, the occasional newer Japanese car, ornate, multicoloured buses and lorries looking like gypsy caravans, pony-traps and bullock carts. We passed the big cannon which Kipling made famous in his novel *Kim*, and, apparently, the largest mosque in the world.

The officials at Gujranwala had done everything possible to make the day go with a swing. There was a plentiful supply of the official World Cup tea and the official World Cup soft drinks but the press must have been glad of the shamianars which shaded their spacious elevated position and we, in a cramped but well-positioned BBC Radio commentary box, were certainly pleased that it was protected from the burning heat of the sun.

It was a sweltering day and when Allan Lamb, with invaluable help from Emburey, DeFreitas and Foster, pulled the chestnuts out of the fire against a West Indies side which hardly deserved to lose, he came off the field absolutely exhausted.

It was obviously a great start to the tournament for England to beat West Indies but the team has clear limitations. Pringle was savaged by Richards, Richardson, Logie, Dujon and Harper, and with Broad out of form and Robinson lacking the necessary thrust and flexibility for 50-overs cricket on slow pitches, they looked unimpressive. The exception was when Gatting and Gooch were together and later when Lamb, the spark of his aggression lit by Emburey, began one of his heroic bursts of hitting.

C.M-J.

Saturday 10 October, Lahore I spent the day at the pleasant Pearl Continental Hotel in Lahore watching David Houghton nearly pulling off an extraordinary victory for Zimbabwe against New Zealand. After packing and paying the bill, we left the hotel at five for a short flight, comfortable apart from some bouncing around in storms which had been breaking heavily around Rawalpindi and its modern twin city, Islamabad. About four hours later we were safely ensconced in Islamabad, the administrative and diplomatic capital of Pakistan, picturesquely sited near the western tip of the Himalayas.

C.M-J.

Sunday 11 October, Islamabad Rain seriously threatens tomorrow's match at 'Pindi between Pakistan and England. Golf at the Islamabad club, with Woodcock, Thicknesse and myself representing the amateurs and Illingworth, Lewis and Bannister the professionals, was cut short after nine holes by thunder and lightning. Illingworth led the professional retreat from the links with Lewis, yellow at the gills from a stomach upset, not far behind. Bannister, well up on both of them, was rather more reluctant to leave, reasoning that a bit of rain never hurt anyone. Thicknesse was leading the amateur threesome from behind but, rather to our surprise, we discovered that between us we had managed 25 stapleford points over the first nine holes and stood all-square with the professional trio.

The weather and the correct balance of England's team have been today's main talking points.

A dramatic thunderstorm broke over Rawalpindi this afternoon and such was the quality of rain and hail that fell, a full 50-overs match tomorrow seems to me to be very unlikely. England were able to practise earlier this afternoon, though could not have a proper net session. Both teams would probably prefer to start the match on Tuesday rather than having to play a reduced game tomorrow. Twenty-five overs is the minimum but if play starts at all tomorrow and rain intervenes the teams would share the points. I dare say both England and Pakistan would settle for two points, but it would also suit the West Indies, who cannot afford to let either of their two main opponents get too far in front.

The pitch at 'Pindi is bone dry, white in colour, hard and true. England won't name a side until the morning but the choice apparently lies between keeping the same XI or playing Eddie Hemmings in place of Derek Pringle. Jarvis and Athey are the two certain absentees, although it is not clear to me why Robinson is preferred to Athey or why Jarvis, who fields better than either Pringle or Hemmings in a side which badly needs sharpening up in the field, is not being given serious consideration. If the weather does allow a proper match, it may yet be another tight finish. Pakistan's theoretical home advantage is perhaps outweighed by the confidence England will have built up after having beaten Pakistan in four of the five Internationals they have played against them this year.

C.M-J.

Monday 12 October, Islamabad A leisurely 7.15 departure this morning. The journey to 'Pindi lasts only half an hour and it was always going to be a forlorn one. The ground was hopelessly wet in areas of the outfield although somehow the pitch itself was dry despite the antiquated covers, which consisted of a couple of polythene sheets and several blankets pinned down by two upturned tables. The *TMS* show had to go on so we filled most of the two and a half hours, before umpires Crafter and Gupta decided to postpone the game for 24 hours, with idle chatter which I suppose must have been better than nothing for those who had switched on Radio 3 at 5.00 a.m. hoping for cricket.

I dined on curry at the pleasant residence of Zakir Husain Syed, Pakistan correspondent of *The Cricketer* and also Deputy Managing Director of the Pakistan Tourist Development Agency. Tourism here has apparently been doubly badly hit by the Iran/Iraq conflict and, worse, the Russian occupation of Afghanistan, which of course has closed the overland route into Pakistan from the north.

Zakir's wife prepared the excellent curry but, according to custom, remained in the kitchen and was not introduced. We spoke of Imran Khan's probable future career in politics and of his opposition to the idea of an arranged marriage with a girl he has never met.

C.M-J.

Tuesday 13 October, Islamabad The postponed match was played in a much more comfortable temperature of around 80 degrees and England contrived to lose it by an inept batting performance against a spirited Pakistan side urged on by the noisiest crowd I can remember anywhere. Although Emburey and Pringle again conceded 50-plus in their ten overs and Salim Malik and Ijaz Ahmed hit some fine shots, England had the great good fortune to be faced with a Pakistan attack devoid of Imran Khan, who had a stomach upset. Perhaps he should stick to eating microwaved baked beans!

Broad and Robinson were too dilatory at the start; Abdul Qadir bowled brilliantly, Wasim Akram and Salim Jaffar exceptionally well and England contrived to lose their last six wickets for 15 runs in a frenzied finish containing three run-outs.

To qualify for a semi-final England must win three of their four remaining matches. The doubts one had about the original selection of the 14 players are

At work in our commentary box at
Rawalpindi.   Graham Morris

proving well-founded. Either Colin Wells or David Capel would have been far more effective with the bat than Pringle and no more expensive with the ball. And both Athey and Robinson are limited batsmen, at their best in three- or five-day cricket. Any two of Fairbrother, Robin Smith, John Morris, Whitaker, Metcalfe or Stewart would have provided the youth and enterprise which is missing.

But they must make the most of the players that are here. On Saturday I would play Jarvis or Hemmings for Pringle, depending on the look of the pitch, and Athey for Robinson, although Broad is also playing without fluency and is slow in the field. Gatting must go in at number three to assert some early purpose and authority. Mind you, one looks to Gooch for this as well. Finally Gatting must think about batting first. Eight matches have now been played and only one of them has been won by the side batting second.

C.M-J.

Wednesday 14 October, Islamabad Some of the England team played golf today but all of them did some hard thinking, I hope, about their bad cricket yesterday. They now need to stop the rot at once with a decisive win over Sri Lanka in Peshawar on Saturday, although they can hardly hope to equal the domination of the West Indies, who must be immensely fortified by Viv Richards' astonishing muscular brilliance in Karachi, watched, incidentally and ironically, by the smallest crowd for any of the matches. England, although they are level on four points with West Indies behind Pakistan in Group B, are going to have to show more character under pressure if they are not to finish third and miss the semi-finals. There *must* be changes to a side which has had one lucky win and one badly-missed opportunity. To have lost to Pakistan without Imran Khan bowling a single ball was to waste a chance which won't come again. The problems which have to be solved are: the weakness of Pringle's bowling against good players on good pitches; the relative ponderousness of some of the fielding; dilatory batting at the start of the innings; and, in yesterday's case, abysmal running between wickets.

C.M-J.

Thursday 15 October, Peshawar The England team flew this evening from Rawalpindi to Peshawar on the North-West Frontier, the press party travelling the 100-odd miles in small buses earlier in the day, a fascinating if sometimes hazardous four-hour journey through the soulless outskirts of Islamabad, on through some remote, rural areas with mud-hut villages and past the wide waters of the Indus, alternately brown and blue, to the seething frontier town of Peshawar with its Pathan population in their cloth headbands swelled by Afghan refugees from the Russian invasion. Kabul is nearer to us now than Lahore.

Soon after booking into our modern hotel, something of an oasis from the bustle outside and boasting a bar for non-Moslems, I went on a hair-raising motor-rickshaw ride to the Shahi Bagh Stadium where the Sri Lankans were arriving for what turned out to be an energetic net session, during which their many batting talents and slimmer bowling resources were on display. In spite of the latter Rumesh Ratnayake looks genuinely quick and may be regaining the rhythm which caused him to hit Larry Gomes in the teeth and Clive Lloyd on the head in Australia a couple of years ago.

The stadium is saucer-shaped with concrete steps all round which are said to hold 20,000 people. There is a palatial pavilion with huge modern dressing-rooms. The pitch is devoid of all grass – it is made of very well baked grey mud which glistens in the sun. I imagine it will be slow and true. All the more reason to play Eddie Hemmings in place of Derek Pringle, although the mountain air will no doubt produce quite an early morning dew which the side bowling first may be able to exploit. The mid-day temperatures here recently, on the other hand, have been nearer 90 than 80.

Elsewhere we have had the first public statements criticising an umpire's decision, namely that of the West Indian David Archer, whom New Zealand believe lost them the match against India by wrongly giving Martin Crowe out stumped by Kiran More. The news from Lahore, where West Indies and Pakistan have a crucial match tomorrow which may determine the outcome of the group, is that Imran Khan is better and should be fit to play.

C.M-J.

Friday 16 October, Peshawar The Pakistan win means that they have to win only one of their three remaining games to be virtually certain of playing in the semi-final in Lahore. England may suffer West Indian vengeance in due course but if they can beat Sri Lanka tomorrow, which is no formality against the holders of the Asia Cup, they will be four points clear of the team which has never previously failed to make the World Cup final.

England will make two changes. Eddie Hemmings will replace Neil Foster, whose injured knee would probably last ten overs but who will need to be 100 per cent fit for later games, and Bill Athey will take over from Tim Robinson, batting at number three if England should lose an early wicket but at six otherwise, with Gatting and Lamb, England's most forceful batsmen apart from Gooch, coming in at three and four. Foster's injury probably means a reprieve for Derek Pringle, and Paul Jarvis wasn't seriously considered because of a shoulder injury which prevented him from having a proper bowl at England's net practice today.

Sri Lanka have a genuinely strong batting team and believe in their ability to beat England. A deafening roar went up from their team-room when they watched Pakistan scramble their victory off the last ball today. They know that if they beat England tomorrow it will be Pakistan in the clear with the other three or four points. England, though, have to think positively. If they can win tomorrow they will relegate West Indies to third place and everyone is aware of the need to leave nothing to chance. It was, for example, only a careless overthrow which allowed Abdul Qadir to take the strike when Jaffer would otherwise have had to take on Walsh in the final over today which brought about the West Indies' defeat. In

Hemmings and Athey England have two very experienced professionals who know what is required.

C.M-J.

Friday 16 October, Peshawar I went to inspect the broadcasting facilities at the Shahi Bagh Stadium this morning and found our room perched high in the brand new pavilion where all the broadcasting boxes open off an ante-room.

Our designated box, however, has been split by a glazed partition. 'Why?' I asked. 'One half is for Sri Lanka Radio', I was told. 'But they're not here', I said. 'No,' came the answer, 'but they want to take your commentary.' This was the first I had heard of that, but I agreed (not that my agreement was being sought) and went on to insist that the glass panel that divided the box should be removed. As is the way in these parts, once the intention is known and the administrative objections have been ignored, the application is easy.

The next problem came later in the afternoon, when one of the PBC engineers came to the hotel to announce that we have no broadcasting circuits to London booked for tomorrow. I immediately agreed to accompany him down to the ground again to try to sort out the problem. Fortunately the local telecom engineer was there with his list of booked communications facilities and there on his list was 'BBC Radio: four-line circuit to London'. 'Where is that?' I asked. 'Oh, BBC Television said they should have it, so it is in their booth.' 'Well, please move it', I insisted.

The task took three hours, mainly because the engineer had to disappear to the mosque for his Friday prayers in the middle of our negotiations. But as the shadows lengthened we sorted out our circuits for London and Colombo and I even managed to solve the problem of BBC Television's missing line without pinching someone else's. And so I wandered back to the hotel past the donkey stables with a tiny farrier's hut, the street chicken-sellers and the barbers perched precariously on planks across a ditch with their customers squatting in front of them. There is a pleasant feel about Peshawar, but tomorrow is an important day for England.

P.B.

Saturday 17 October, Peshawar A satisfactory day for England who overwhelmed Sri Lanka at Peshawar. Having won the toss, for the third time, Mike Gatting on this occasion had the wisdom to bat first on a slow but dead true pitch, and although Broad again struggled to get on top, Gooch, Gatting, Lamb and Emburey all took full toll of Sri Lanka's modest attack. Once they had lost three wickets Sri Lanka were never in the hunt, and although rain reduced their target, England's only concern was that 25 overs should be completed to ensure a valid match.

Sri Lanka did not show in this game what they are undoubtedly capable of but it is hard to see them winning many Test matches with the attack they now have. England, on the other hand, produced their best cricket so far and the inclusion of both Hemmings and Athey was an improvement.

C.M-J.

The Shahi Bagh Stadium, Peshawar   Peter Baxter

Sunday 18 October, Islamabad The England team flew from Peshawar to Karachi on a direct flight while the 'media' party went by coach to Islamabad – a comfortable and picturesque retracing of our steps the other day – and then flew on to Karachi, arriving at about 10.00 p.m. after a pleasant flight, and clocking in at the most luxurious Pearl Continental Hotel.

Usually travel days tend to be wasted but I managed to get some work done, postcards written and even squeezed in nine delightful holes of golf at the attractive Islamabad club. My golf was less impressive than the course, but that was my fault, except for one hole where the caddy assured me I could drive over a tree to the 'blind' green. I hit it as well as I could and ended deep in a wadi in the middle of the trees well over 200 yards away. The consensus was that not even Seve Ballesteros would have attempted the shot!

C.M-J.

Monday 19 October, Karachi A most unfortunate accident to Paul Downton during practice in Karachi this morning has threatened England's chances of getting the win they need to share the leadership of Group B by beating Pakistan tomorrow. Downton was standing some 70 yards away from Phillip DeFreitas, batting in the nets, when he was hit by a flat, skimming drive flush on the left cheek bone. A large swelling like a carbuncle immediately appeared underneath his eye and although an X-ray has shown no fracture there must be a danger that Downton will not be able to see clearly tomorrow and that Bill Athey, a very occasional wicketkeeper, will have to take over. I spoke to Downton late this afternoon and his eye was at least half-closed and very sore.

If Downton is fit, England will probably make two changes, bringing back Foster, whose knee injury seems better, for Pringle and Robinson for Broad, who has not been able to get going on the slow pitches. With two spinners now in the England attack and another bare mud pitch expected to turn a little, the difficulty for an inexperienced 'keeper will be exaggerated. Pakistan are expected to be unchanged although they would surely be strengthened if they brought in Mudassar Nazar for Mansoor Akhtar.

England beat Pakistan on neutral territory in One-Day Internationals earlier this year in Perth and won the Texaco Trophy at home by the odd game in three and the skin of their teeth. But home advantage played a definite part in the result in Rawalpindi the other day when England's panicky collapse and ultimate failure had at least something to do with the uproarious support for the home team. A crowd of almost twice the size – in other words a capacity 35,000 – can confidently be expected tomorrow and if Mike Gatting should win his fourth toss out of four I would expect him to bat first this time and leave the extra pressure which is felt by any team having to chase a target of much more than four an over to his opponents.

Remembering the crowd disturbance which erupted at Edgbaston during that extraordinarily tense game earlier this year, Imran and Gatting would be well advised to get together before this match to agree to no exhibitions from either team which might incite violence from a notoriously volatile crowd. Karachi has been the scene of more than one riot in recent years and a repetition of the Miandad lbw incident could lead to trouble which no one wants. Another large police presence on the ground will be designed to nip any such nonsense in the bud. Today they were combing the outfield with metal detectors.

C.M-J.

Sweeping the outfield in Karachi for mines
as Mike Gatting reviews the troops.

Peter Baxter

Wednesday 21 October, Karachi England and Pakistan have reacted very differently to the match which saw the home team stride into the semi-finals and left England, in view of the West Indies victory over Sri Lanka today, having to win against West Indies on Monday at Jaipur. Curiously enough this was a repeat of the situation in the much less important World Series Cup in Australia earlier this year when England won the crunch match with the West Indies at Devonport in Tasmania and went on to win the whole competition.

While Pakistan refused to rest on their laurels, which range from lavish monetary gifts from rich businessmen to the players to official messages of congratulation from the President, General Zia-ul-Haq, in which he notes the support of Allah for Pakistan, England had a complete day off today. By contrast Pakistan had a hard three-hour practice session at the Karachi Gymkhana club, the old Test ground here.

I don't blame England for taking a day off today after a hard match but I understand that they are not practising again till Saturday, and when you think they could have an enforced two weeks of inactivity before the second leg of their Pakistan tour if they fail to make the semi-finals, this seems an unwise relaxation at a time when the players have to be kept fully tuned.

Of course, if England lose on Monday there is still a chance that they could get to the semi-final on run-rate by dint of a second Pakistan victory over West Indies in their last match, but England would then be required to beat Sri Lanka by a more comfortable margin than the West Indies managed today. In short, England are in no position to take it easy.

C.M-J.

Thursday 22 October, Delhi After a certain amount of chin-wagging about whether or not to make use of better practice facilities in Karachi than will be available to them when they get to Jaipur, this morning nine of the England party of 14 decided to make the short journey from their hotel to the Gymkhana club, which – apart from the fact that its members drink lemonade rather than gin and tonic – has not changed since Partition in 1947.

There was certainly a beautiful net wicket right in the middle of the ground and Tim Robinson, in particular, made the most of it. Robinson's Nottinghamshire friend and rival Chris Broad was rather less impressive, I'm afraid, and after all his success last winter he is going through the kind of worrying loss of form that has afflicted many a good player before now. Remember Denis Compton in Australia in 1950-51 and Peter May in South Africa in 1956-57; two of England's greatest post-war batsmen, neither of whom knew for a time where their next decent score was coming from?

Broad may not be quite in that exalted class but, like Dennis Amiss, who couldn't get a run in India in 1972-73 but then scored an avalanche of them for England once he had found his touch in Pakistan, Broad too will solve his problem. For the moment though he has to be ruled out of England's XI for Monday. The plan is for England to practise properly on Saturday after the journey to Jaipur tomorrow. We all arrived in Delhi at about 9.15 Indian time this evening and there is quite a jolly atmosphere in the capital, with fireworks lighting up the sky to celebrate the Hindu festival of Diwali and no fewer than four of the World Cup teams under the same roof tonight. This is a friendly tournament as well as a competitive one.

C.M-J.

Friday 23 October, Delhi The England and West Indian teams travelled on the same Indian Airways 'plane this evening on the short flight from Delhi to Jaipur, and for such a naturally exuberant bunch the West Indies, who are in only the early stages of a long tour in India, were in a rather subdued mood, very aware no doubt of the fact that in six one-day matches against England this year they have somehow lost five. What is more, without Joel Garner and Malcolm Marshall they are not so strong a team as they were in Australia last winter.

The sight of Tony Gray of Trinidad and Surrey towering over everyone else, however, made one wonder why West Indies have continued not to use him when he is fit again and a very good bowler indeed to leave out. All is not lost for West Indies yet, though, and the form of Viv Richards has been ominously good. If he plays a major innings in Jaipur on Monday England are unlikely to win. Richards is even more vital to West Indies now than Clive Lloyd was to the first World Cup champions of 1975.

England's preparations for this climactic match on Monday began in earnest this morning in Delhi with an energetic workout at the National Stadium from which everyone emerged fit for selection. Micky Stewart paid particular attention to the fielding, which was not at its best against Pakistan in Karachi, not just because two catches went down but also because the throwing to Paul Downton was not as accurate as it should have been. Little things count in a game as short as 50 overs and there will be no margin for error here in Jaipur on Monday.

C.M-J.

Friday 23 October, Delhi We are back in India at something of a World Cup crossroads in Delhi's Taj Palace Hotel. Last night it housed the teams from England – en route from Karachi to Jaipur; the West Indies – also going to Jaipur, but from Kanpur; Sri Lanka – en route from Kanpur back to Pakistan and Faisalabad, and Australia and India, who had been playing the day before in Delhi. For Christopher and me it was good especially to catch up with Henry Blofeld and Trevor Bailey before we go our separate ways; they to Chandigarh, we to the pink city of Jaipur, whose Maharajahs built so many fine buildings including the Amber Palace, the Hawar Mahal and the hotel we are to stay in: the magnificent Rambagh Palace.

P.B.

Saturday 24 October, Jaipur After watching England's practice session at Jaipur on beautiful net wickets with some grass on them allowing a little bit of pace and

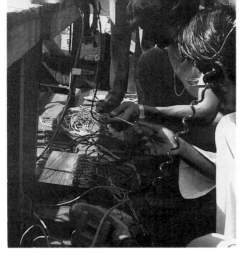

*'One of these wires must go to London!
Technical expertise in operation in Jaipur.*
Peter Baxter

bounce (Tony Gray later broke his arm batting against, of all people, Carl Hooper), I sat at our match commentary position with Peter Baxter getting grilled in a temperature of 100 degrees – in the shade, which we only partially were – while technicians jabbered away and fiddled with wires all round us. They had started far too late in their attempts to get a line to the ground from their local GPO and in the end the circuit came up an hour late. I missed my live contribution to *Sport on Four* but successfully linked with Trevor Bailey in Delhi for a resumé of the tournament so far. I said that England would beat West Indies on Monday unless Viv Richards makes a hundred!

In the afternoon I took part in an eccentric, parching but amusing game of golf with Lewis, Selvey, Woodcock and Thicknesse on a course made purely of desert sand apart from a couple of holes across Jaipur's famous polo field. Each shot from the fairway is played off a small mat carried by the caddies who also sweep the 'browns' before you putt. If you go into the rough, which looks exactly like the 'fairway', you improve your bunker play!

Indian beer, not the country's finest product, has never tasted better than it did after this.

C.M-J.

Sunday 25 October, Jaipur A languid day in the intense heat, catching up on scorecards, statistics and letters. I write this diary entry sitting in a cane chair, shaded from a totally cloudless azure sky by an arched roof held up by carved marble pillars. Behind me on a lawn a young Indian in a yellow turban is blowing monotonously on a pipe with a 12-foot cobra slithering round his neck and a smaller one rising up in front on him, looking not so much charmed as bored. Another beturbaned Indian sits in the lotus position 50 yards beyond under a blue parasol, strumming away on a sitar which he sometimes changes for a rather tuneless fiddle. Butterflies and the occasional vivid green parrot flit among the trees and bougainvillaea across the extensive lawns which run away from the symmetrical splendour of the yellow stone palace. There is a smell of curry on the hot breeze, but I do not feel like lunch.

C.M-J.

Monday 26 October, Jaipur The day after the match against Pakistan in Karachi, I had to have something of a rethink about our commentary team. Sharing duties for Jack Bannister and Tony Lewis with television, which was accepted as perfectly viable in London before we came out, is now proving impractical. It culminated in Karachi in the abrupt removal of Tony in mid-over. Jack, too, was restricted by both television and newspaper commitments. I scratched my head and came up with an idea. Tim Rice. The successful creator of *Jesus Christ Superstar* and *Evita* is travelling with us as a cricket fan, pure and simple. But he is used to broadcasting, can use words and I was confident that he would not let us down, with good summarisers like Mike Selvey and Peter Roebuck to nurse him through any technical difficulties. When I rang his room with the invitation he thought first that he was dreaming and then that it was a bad joke. But today his day came and as we made our way to the Sawai Man Singh Stadium he was, if not quite as nervous as on one of his first nights, then not far from it. He need not have worried.

P.B.

Monday 26 October, Jaipur England beat the West Indies again, the sixth time out of seven this year. Amazing! Tim Rice made an understandably nervous but brave and conscientious guest appearance as a *TMS* commentator, in lieu of Lewis and Bannister, who had been claimed by television on the other side of the big and beautiful ground. Graham Gooch made a staunch and heartening 92 on a pitch which was distinctly juicy early on. Walsh was unlucky but Patterson wayward, and England were lucky that Gray was injured and Baptiste not selected.

Richards batted superbly and Richardson brilliantly at times, luckily at others. But admirable bowling by Emburey and Hemmings and DeFreitas did the trick in a game which kept one guessing until the last few overs. This has given a tremendous fillip to the England tour. The win means a semi-final place, barring an accident against Sri Lanka on Friday, and saves the players the embarrassment of having to spend a fortnight's holiday in Goa before the second leg of the tour.

C.M-J.

Tuesday 27 October, Bombay We had our first real communications nightmare today. Our Jaipur to Bombay flight was held up for three hours, not reaching base until 2.00 a.m. I made an abortive dash back into the town with John Woodcock to try to warn the BBC by telex that I might not get through for the 6.45 programme. There was no question of getting a telephone call through from the airport.

By hovering near the departure desk on our return to the airport, however, we gathered that there might be a few spare seats on the direct flight to Bombay which the team were taking, and a bit of luck and initiative got us on. Three other journalists jumped on the same bandwagon, much to the disgust of their colleagues, who made sure the early arrivals (11.30 p.m.) were given a five o'clock early morning call, but at least I got my report through.

C.M-J.

Wednesday 28 October, Bombay Firmly resolved not to make any mistake on Friday in their last qualifying match against Sri Lanka, nine of the England team used what otherwise might have been a wasted day to practise this morning at the Wankhede Stadium where – if all goes well – England will play their semi-final against India or Australia next Wednesday – tomorrow week.

Eddie Hemmings was resting after his heroic exertions in Jaipur, but four players were unable to take part because of injuries and a fifth, the luckless Paul Jarvis, was able to bowl for only 15 minutes before his injured right shoulder became too painful. Any thought of playing him has probably now been abandoned.

The other injuries are bruised fingers in the cases of Gatting and Athey, a thigh strain affecting John Emburey and, perhaps most serious, a shoulder injury to Allan Lamb, whose strong throwing from deep cover or mid-wicket is an important part of England's strategy.

Micky Stewart tried an interesting experiment with his seam bowlers this morning, getting them to bowl in the nets in six-ball overs. Concentration is as important to bowling as it is to batting and, as the West Indies proved on Monday, inaccurate bowling is fatal in these hectic 50-overs matches. England are due in Poona late tonight after the short evening flight from Bombay.

C.M-J.

Friday 30 October, Poona Sri Lanka (218-7) lost to England (219-2) by 8 wickets. England made sure of their semi-final place when Sri Lanka, a weary and travel-worn team, failed to take advantage of batting first for the first time in their six matches. It was really no contest once Tim Robinson and Graham Gooch, the latter making light of a dislocated finger suffered when he dropped Ratneyeke off a sharp slip chance in the first over, had put on 123 in 23 overs for the first wicket in response to an inadequate Sri Lankan total on yet another comfortable wicket.

Gooch won the 'man of the match' award but Robinson, who was in his element on a slow pitch against straightforward bowling, was at least as deserving a winner, especially since he had fielded particularly well. England's ground-fielding on an outfield which was a sad mixture of grass and dry mud was good, but four catches were missed, the worst a simple outside edge to Downton by Dias off Small when Sri Lanka's vice-captain had scored only one. He stayed, happily, to show the complete range of strokes of which he is capable, hitting three sixes, one a quite extraordinary wristy force off the back foot over mid-wicket off Small. The tall left-hander, Gurusinhe, also had a good day, revealing his power and promise in a commendable third-wicket stand which had England, if not worried, at least anxious. Later, Jeganathan and Anurasiri were the best of Sri Lanka's bowlers, the former flighting it nicely and being rewarded with both England wickets.

Small was the pick of England's bowlers on a day when Foster and Hemmings were not at their best, and DeFreitas and Emburey confirmed their position as England's most reliable bowlers.

C.M-J.

Saturday 31 October, Poona After all the palpitations and a high proportion of close finishes, the Reliance World Cup's qualifying games produced few genuine surprises and the four semi-finalists who emerged are those most of us expected. India and Australia came through from Group A, although only in that order as a result of India's barn-storming finish on Saturday, when the reigning champions were seen in their most dazzling light. Such is the national fervour now sweeping India on that it will be hard indeed for England to stop their momentum in Bombay on Thursday. It was equally to be expected that Pakistan would win Group B and England settled the question of who would go through with them by virtue of their two victories over West Indies.

Whatever happens on Thursday and, indeed, during the remainder of the winter's activities, these tests of both strength and character will stand England in good stead when Viv Richards brings a tired and reinforced team to England in 1988. By then West Indies will have played tough series away against India and at home to Pakistan. England will have played series against Pakistan and New Zealand. It will be interesting to see which of the two teams that faced each other in Gujranwala and Jaipur will walk out again at Trent Bridge next June.

C.M-J.

Sunday 1 November, Bombay We came by train – the Deccan Queen – from Poona to Bombay. There were some scenes of desperate poverty in both places. Goodness knows how many millions – yes, millions – of Indians have no roof over their heads or, at best, a stinking hovel. We also passed, however, many fertile, well-ordered fields, some being ploughed by bullock-teams, in the plains between the well-vegetated hills.

Bombay was smelly and very hot when we arrived. The Taj Mahal Hotel was, as always, a welcome haven, but my decision to eat fish for dinner was probably the reason for painful, enervating and frighteningly violent bouts of diarrhoea through most of the night. Modern medicine eventually triumphed over the all too familiar consequences of inadequate hygiene and a polluted sea. Or was it the filthy coffee cup on the Deccan Queen? At the nadir of my excruciating gripes I vowed never to come to India again. But necessity and the country's many fascinations will no doubt draw me back.

C.M-J.

Monday 2 November, Bombay The England team practised at the Wankhede Stadium today in high humidity and a temperature of just on 100 degrees fahrenheit. Thursday's match is going to be exhausting and this is no weather in which to be out if you are unwell which is why Sunil Gavaskar, who made his brilliant hundred against New Zealand on Saturday despite running a temperature, missed the Indian practice and spent the day in bed.

England's main worry at the moment is Neil Foster's sore right knee. He ran about today but didn't bowl and Derek Pringle stands by to replace him if necessary, although this would inevitably lessen England's chances. On these bland pitches Pringle is unfortunately innocuous whereas Foster, although he still bowls too many loose deliveries, does also produce the wicket-taking ball.

The tactics of all the captains in this tournament have been stereotyped and all of them would do well to remember that taking a wicket is the best way of stopping any batsman scoring runs. Whereas a 40-overs International between India and Sri Lanka here last January produced 588 runs, the game between India and Zimbabwe a fortnight ago was the only really low-scoring match in the tournament. On that occasion Zimbabwe collapsed early against Prabhakar and the pitch as it was this morning after a watering yesterday was damp enough to make batting first a hazard, despite the overwhelming evidence that to get the runs on the board is an advantage.

C.M-J.

Tuesday 3 November, Bombay Both teams expect to be at full strength for the first semi-final between Pakistan and Australia in Lahore and one need hardly say that the weather is set fair and that there will be a full house, the vast majority of spectators expecting Pakistan to reach the World Cup final for the first time.

The game has been described by Allan Border as a battle between Australia's batting and Pakistan's bowling. This is one way of looking at it, but another is to examine the theoretical weaknesses of the two teams: here there is not much doubt that Pakistan's batting is stronger than Australia's bowling. Craig McDermott, with 11 wickets at 20 is the only Australian bowler who has what one might term impressive figures, although Steve Waugh twice bowled very well in the crucial final stages of the preliminary games. Pakistan, by contrast, have two world-class bowlers who have lived up to expectations: Imran Khan with 14 wickets at 13 each and Abdul Qadir with 12 at 16. Tauseef, who is recovering from 'flu, has bowled economically and there is relief that Wasim Akram's bruised toe will not prevent him playing a crucial part both with the new ball and in the later stages.

Australia's great hope, no doubt, is to win the toss and get the sort of commanding start that Marsh and Boon have consistently been giving them. Marsh has hit two of only five centuries in the competition so far and Boon has also scored over 300 runs: Marsh averages 74, Boon 51. Pakistan must be uncomfortably aware that Border has scored only 134 from six innings. When last he played in Lahore in the Test match of 1983 he scored 150 not out and 153.

Pakistan have to decide whether to open their batting with Mudassar or Mansoor. It would be a surprise if they did not use Mudassar's vast experience and he must be a better fifth bowler than Salim Malik. A high-scoring match seems certain and if Pakistan are worthy favourites it is only by a shade of odds.

The news from the Indian and England camps today is that Sunil Gavaskar is better after his fever although not yet 100 per cent fit and that Neil Foster, as he told me this afternoon, is now more hopeful of playing on Thursday.

C.M-J.

Thursday 5 November, Bombay Having shaken off my violent tummy bug I am now in the grip of a more orthodox 'flu/cold type virus so my commentaries cannot have been at their most lucid today; a pity because England excelled themselves to defeat India and so, after Pakistan's failure to justify favouritism over Australia in Lahore yesterday, it will be England versus Australia in the final on Sunday.

The common denominator of the two semi-finals was that the side which batted first won, and I would bet now that the side which bats first in Calcutta will win again. At Bombay it was Kapil Dev's choice to put England in, one he will bitterly regret. The ball did not swing as he had hoped on a muggy day and, thanks to a brilliant century by Graham Gooch, given excellent support by Gatting and Lamb, England built a score which was out of India's reach. The pitch – rust-coloured – was turning all through the game and Maninder Singh had Robinson stumped with a lovely, old-fashioned piece of slow left-arm bowling before being swept to distraction by Gooch and, to a lesser extent, Gatting.

It looked as though India would, after all, get the runs when Kapil Dev built on some good early work by Srikkanth, Azharuddin and Pandit with a dazzling piece of hitting, but Hemmings kept his head and Kapil holed out to Gatting at mid-wicket. Having gone for 26 in his first three overs, Hemmings finished with four wickets and he and his team-mates are for the moment in seventh heaven.

C.M-J.

Friday 6 November The England team are all smiles this morning after their great victory, and they have worked for it. India's cricket press took a balanced view, on the whole, acknowledging that England simply played better. That there is wide-spread disappointment, though, cannot be hidden, certainly not by the former president of the Indian Board, Mr Salve, who offered no direct hospitality yesterday to the president of the ICC, J.J. Warr, or the other English officials present, and who asked Mr Allan Rea of the West Indies Cricket Board, rather than the ICC president, to present the prizes in what may have been a deliberate slight. Mr Salve felt himself to have been cold-shouldered when MCC officials were unable to get extra tickets for his colleagues at the 1983 final.

Generally, however, the Indian reaction was magnanimous and far from sour. The only Indo-Pakistan presence on the field in Sunday's final will be that of the umpires, Ram Bapu Gupta from India and Mahboob Shah from Pakistan. Allan Border's request that Dickie Bird and Tony Crafter should stand was not accepted by the organising committee and one can well understand why.

England will practise in Calcutta tomorrow after travelling there this evening. Advance word is that the pitch may be no better than the one in Bombay, but 450 runs were scored in the only previous match in the tournament to be held there, so I shall be surprised if batsmen do not continue to prosper.

For psychological reasons, and because Bruce Reid prefers bowling to right-handers, England may think of bringing back Chris Broad for Tim Robinson. Incidentally Paul Jarvis, the only man in the 14 not to have had a game, is now hopeful of being fully fit for the rest of the tour. Gladstone Small would stay on if Jarvis were to fail a thorough fitness test next week.

The game between the World Cup champions and the rest of the world which had been planned in Calcutta for next Tuesday has been cancelled – a decision which has delighted the players of all teams, who feel they have played quite enough 50-overs cricket for the time being.

The vast disappointment of a fair proportion of India's 800 million people was obvious from a number of little things. The lobby of the famous Taj Mahal Hotel at Bombay was much less full after the match than it had been on the eve of the semi-final. Had India won, there would have been no room to move. Indian cricketers are demi-gods; they really are worshipped. This time the idols had feet of clay and it was time for them to retreat behind hotel doors before leaving quietly this morning for their homes in different parts of India, while the England team left for the airport by coach, the object of a thousand fascinated stares. The airport too was emptier than usual. Thousands of seats to Calcutta were suddenly vacant.

But the route to the airport through Bombay's crowded streets provided evidence aplenty that cricket will not in any way be set back by India's failure – if such it is – to reach the final. Last time I was in Barbados I thought the traditional story of a game of cricket around every corner had sadly become a bit of a myth, but in Bombay the absolute passion for the game is everywhere to be seen.

The Gymkhana ground, an area about the size of Lord's and the Nursery put together, must have had ten separate games going on simultaneously as the sun began to set. This was the ground from which a boy came home one evening and proudly told his mother that he had taken five catches – but none in the match in which he was playing! Less formal games of cricket were going on everywhere, tiny children with tiny bats playing away in the twilight amid the filth and dust of the pavements or the dried mud backyards of their makeshift slum dwellings. There was even a game being played on a roundabout in the middle of the traffic in an area that can't have been more than five square yards.

With such enthusiasm, undampened by their latest defeat, the Indian team can only continue to be one of the best in the world. The sad thing, though, is that only a tiny proportion of those youngsters playing in the streets will get the chance to play organised cricket at school. Most will remain too poor to own proper equipment, although for a lucky few the game may hold the key to undreamed riches.

C.M-J.

Sunday 8 November, Calcutta The final of the World Cup was an extraordinary event. The ground looked superb, an imposing and inspiring stage, dressed to the nines for the big occasion. A crowd approaching 90,000 thoroughly enjoyed their day, many of them able to forget for a few hours the misery in which they live much of their lives, and at the end they cheered Australia with as much fervour as they would have India. Thunderous fireworks and a parade of past players in open jeeps completed a spectacular occasion.

The packed Eden Gardens, Calcutta.   Graham Morris

I was terribly ill throughout the day, with a high temperature and nausea, having spent the previous night in the bathroom, so sadly what should have been an unforgettable memory will for me personally only be a miserable one. Automatic pilot took over as far as the commentating went, but Henry Blofeld did more than his fair share with even more enthusiasm than ever, ending with a 30-minute monologue of breathless encomiums to Australia, Pakistan and India. He was in tremendous form, and so were Allan Border's Australians who, by winning the toss and getting a good score on the board, always looked the likely winners.

England, with DeFreitas having an indifferent day and Small a bad one, gave Boon too much freedom at the start and the rugged little Tasmanian played the major innings, with support from Marsh, Jones and, in a crucial acceleration at the end, Border and Veletta.

Foster bowled superbly to keep England in the match and Emburey and Hemmings both did their best again to keep the target as low as 254. McDermott hustled out Robinson in his first over, but Gooch, Athey, Gatting and Lamb, without ever quite taking control, kept everyone guessing.

A fine spell by O'Donnell helped Australia and then, as England threw their bats in an exciting climax, Waugh produced a superbly accurate spell. The final fling by DeFreitas produced 15 runs from four balls but it was Australia's game in the end, by seven runs. They shared their triumph with the many hard-working people in Pakistan and India who had made the World Cup an outstanding success.

C.M-J.

SUMMARISED SCORES

England in the World Cup

At Gujranwala (Pakistan) 9 October England beat West Indies by 2 wickets

 West Indies 243 for 7 (50 overs) (Richardson 53)
 England 246 for 8 (49.3 overs) (Lamb 67 n o)

At Rawalpindi (Pakistan) 13 October Pakistan beat England by 18 runs

 Pakistan 239 for 7 (50 overs) (Salim Malik 65; Ejaz Ahmed 59)
 England 221 (48.4 overs) (Abdul Qadir 4-31)

At Peshawar (Pakistan) 17 October England beat Sri Lanka on a faster scoring rate

 England 296 for 4 (50 overs) (Gooch 84; Lamb 76; Gatting 58)
 Sri Lanka 158 for 8 (45 overs)

At Karachi (Pakistan) 20 October Pakistan beat England by 7 wickets

 England 244 for 9 (50 overs) (Athey 86; Gatting 60; Imran 4-37)
 Pakistan 247 for 3 (49 overs) Rameez Raja 113; Salim Malik 88)

At Jaipur (India) 26 October England beat West Indies by 34 runs

 England 269 for 5 (50 overs) (Gooch 92)
 West Indies 235 (48.1 overs) (Richardson 93; Richards 51)

At Poona (India) 30 October England beat Sri Lanka by 8 wickets

 Sri Lanka 218 for 7 (50 overs) (Dias 80)
 England 219 for 2 (41.2 overs) (Gooch 61; Robinson 55)

Group B Table	*P*	*W*	*L*	*Pts*
Pakistan	6	5	1	20
England	6	4	2	16
West Indies	6	3	3	12
Sri Lanka	6	0	6	0

Group A Table	*P*	*W*	*L*	*Pts*
India	6	5	1	20
Australia	6	5	1	20
New Zealand	6	2	4	8
Zimbabwe	6	0	6	0

First semi-final at Lahore (Pakistan) 4 November Australia beat Pakistan by 18 runs

 Australia 267 for 8 (50 overs) (Boon 65)
 Pakistan 249 (49 overs) (Javed Miandad 70; Imran Khan 58; McDermott 5-44)

Second semi-final at Bombay (India) 5 November England beat India by 35 runs

ENGLAND				INDIA		
G.A. Gooch	c Srikkanth b Maninder	115		K. Srikkanth	b Foster	31
R.T. Robinson	st More b Maninder	13		S.M. Gavaskar	b DeFreitas	4
C.W.J. Athey	c More b Sharma	4		N.S. Sidhu	c Athey b Foster	22
M.W. Gatting *	b Maninder	56		M. Azharuddin	lbw Hemmings	64
A.J. Lamb	not out	32		C.S. Pandit	lbw b Foster	24
J.E. Emburey	lbw b Kapil Dev	6		Kapil Dev *	c Gatting b Hemmings	30
P.A.J. DeFreitas	b Kapil Dev	7		R.J. Shastri	c Downton b Hemmings	21
P.R. Downton †	not out	1		K.S. More †	c & b Emburey	0
Extras	(b 1, lb 18, w 1)	20		M. Prabhakar	c Downton b Small	4
				C. Sharma	c Lamb b Hemmings	0
TOTAL (50 overs)	6 wkts	254		Maninder Singh	not out	0
				Extras	(b 1, lb 9, w 6, nb 3)	19

Did not bat: N.A. Foster, G.C. Small, E.E. Hemmings.

Fall of wickets: 40, 79, 196, 203, 219, 231.

Bowling: Kapil Dev 10-1-38-2; Prabhakar 9-1-40-0; Maninder Singh 10-0-54-3; Sharma 9-0-41-1; Shastri 10-0-49-0; Azharuddin 2-0-13-0.

Umpires: A.R. Crafter and S.J. Woodward.

TOTAL (45.3 overs) 219

Fall of wickets: 7, 58, 73, 121, 168, 204, 205, 218, 219.

Bowling: DeFreitas 7-0-37-1; Small 6-0-22-1; Emburey 10-1-35-1; Foster 10-0-47-3; Hemmings 9.3-1-52-4; Gooch 3-0-16-0.

Final at Calcutta (India) 8 November Australia beat England by 7 runs

AUSTRALIA				ENGLAND		
D.C. Boon	c Downton b Hemmings	75		G.A. Gooch	lbw b O'Donnell	35
G.R. Marsh	b Foster	24		R.T. Robinson	lbw b McDermott	0
D.M. Jones	c Athey b Hemmings	33		C.W.J. Athey	run out	58
C.J. McDermott	b Gooch	14		M.W. Gatting *	c Dyer b Border	41
A.R. Border *	run out	31		A.J. Lamb	b Waugh	45
M.R.J. Veletta	not out	45		P.R. Downton †	c O'Donnell b Border	9
S.R. Waugh	not out	5		J.E. Emburey	run out	10
Extras	(b 1, lb 13, w 5, nb 7)	26		P.A.J. DeFreitas	c Reid b Waugh	17
				N.A. Foster	not out	7
TOTAL (50 overs)	5 wkts	253		G.C. Small	not out	3
				Extras	(b 1, lb 14, w 3, nb 3)	21

Did not bat: S.P. O'Donnell, G.C. Dyer†, T.B.A. May, B.A. Reid.

Fall of wickets: 75, 151, 166, 168, 241.

Bowling: DeFreitas 6-1-34-0; Small 6-0-33-0; Foster 10-0-38-1; Hemmings 10-1-48-2;

Umpires: R.B. Gupta and Mehboob Shah.

TOTAL (50 overs) 8 wkts 246

Did not bat: E.E. Hemmings.

Fall of wickets: 1, 66, 135, 170, 188, 218, 220, 235.

Bowling: McDermott 10-1-51-1; Reid 10-0-43-0; Waugh 9-0-37-2; O'Donnell 10-1-35-1; May 4-0-27-0; Border 7-0-38-2

Blowers and The Boil in India

Henry Blofeld, Trevor Bailey

After a week of exploration which included two nights in Agra, where the beauty and perfection of the Taj Mahal defies description, Greta, my wife, and I arrived in a Madras hotel. For one magical moment we thought we were back in pre-war India, as waiters scurried hither and thither attending to the wants of an elegant figure, sporting a cravat which was straight out of Somerset Maugham. We watched entranced, until he said, while dispensing largesse, 'My dear old thing, a little more ice in my Scotch'. We then knew we had found Henry. The intention was that Henry and I would supply the BBC with some accounts of the events in India, while the main commentary would be on the England team, based in Pakistan.

Having experienced the perils of a trip to the Madras cricket club by motorised rickshaw, I organised a car to take Henry, Alan Lee, the newly-appointed cricket correspondent of the 'Thunderer', and I to the ground at 7.45 a.m. It was slightly different from travelling to a match in England, as we encountered nine cows, seven water buffaloes, a wide assortment of goats, hens, dogs, pigs and one elephant. We also came within inches of hitting at least 20 other vehicles and failed by the narrowest of margins to bag at least a dozen pedestrians and eight cyclists.

T.B.

I must admit right away that travelling round India with Trevor Bailey, hereinafter to be known as The Boil, was a progress which was as priceless as it was princely and that while the administration was looked after by the Memsahib, Mrs Bailey, it was, too, a smooth progress. After her return to England it became a trifle more problematic. We were, of course, very much the Second XI for the number one correspondents, the First XI, were with England in Pakistan. Our small party was swelled for a long time by Alan Lee, Chris Florence of the BBC World Service and Matthew Engel of the *Guardian* who flitted in and out between journeys to Simla and Lahore and an abortive attempt to penetrate Bangladesh.

During the Lord's Test match the previous June we had been visited in the commentary box by His Highness the Maharajah of Baroda who is a former member of the *TMS* team. In the course of his visit I appointed him as my sub-continental travel agent and he was going to arrange my progress. Alas, noblesse was unable to oblige because the Prince was struck down by ill health and I arrived in India hotel-less. I had a great piece of luck, though, for when I got to Madras for the first match in Group A between India and Australia I ran into an old friend, the former Indian Test all-rounder, M.L. Jaisimha. He solved all my problems by enlisting the help of the Indian team manager who agreed to make all my hotel bookings throughout India. Many of the hotels were already full up, but I found myself squeezed in when others were turned away.

Just before I left London I had picked up from Broadcasting House a tape recorder, a microphone and a most exciting little contraption called a 'Mutter Box' which was to stretch my technical know-how. I was unaware that I should also have collected an alternative schedule to the massive tome I had already been sent by Peter Baxter for our broadcasting duties in India. It proved to be a crucial mistake.

Trevor and I set out for the Chepauk Stadium in Madras ready to commentate as and when we were wanted by London on India's game with Australia. *TMS* proper, led by C.M-J., were doing ball-by-ball from Gujranwala where England were playing the West Indies, but they were going to take quick flashes and inserts from us during the day.

The Boil, Alan Lee and I left the Connemara Hotel at 7.45 a.m., which was a fairly ungodly hour. The Boil had booked a car through the hotel to pick us up in the evening at the same spot at which it deposited us in the morning. It seemed a major success for Bailey Travel. It took just under a quarter of an hour to get to the ground where it was the usual Indian turmoil. Millions of police were blowing whistles and frantically gesticulating, there was a constant blare of car horns and thousands of people were milling about everywhere. We had managed to get a car pass and so after initial opposition from the police we were allowed to drive into a park which was the other side of the ground from the press box. Our driver, amid much nodding of heads, promised to be at the same place at six o'clock, and full of confidence we walked round to the members' entrance.

After The Boil had staked a claim in the press box, he pointed to the back of the stand and to the many broadcasting points. We climbed to the back and after a number of enquiries were shown to a concrete staircase which took us higher still to two more boxes in the rafters. One was for the BBC. After much handshaking I was told that the BBC did not want a line until 4.30 for close of play reports. My schedule clearly stated that a line had been booked from 9.15 to 5.30. I told them without mincing my words that they had got it wrong and the chaps in charge couldn't have been more helpful. In no time at all I was talking on the telephone to the Indian equivalent of Telecom who said they would do what they could.

I was then told by an official that I would have to see the match co-ordinator as there was the question of rights. I suggested that he should come up and see me, but was told that he was an old man and that I would have to go to him. I insisted that The Boil came with me and we were led downstairs to some offices at the back of the stand and met the co-ordinator, Ranga Chara, a man well into his 70s. He had apparently toured Australia under Vijay Hazare in 1947-48. Before getting down to business the three of us talked cricket for a minute or two. Then the old boy said that if we were intending to do commentary or live reports the BBC had to pay for the rights. I understood him to say that it would be $1,000 for the two games in Madras although it turned out to be $1,000 for each match. He insisted that we sign a guarantee saying that BBC would pay the organising committee the appropriate amount. Boil and I had a quick word and thought that we should sign, for the BBC had planned the coverage of the Indian group around us and were not paying us to do nothing. Ranga Chara now dictated at high speed a contract, which he happened to have on the tip of his tongue, to an aide who scribbled it down in longhand. It was the 'We, the undersigned . . .' sort of thing and Boil and I signed it. This was followed by more shaking of heads and hands. The document was rushed out of the room and we were asked to wait. We chatted some more about cricket and it was revealed that Ranga Chara had once bowled Bradman. There was something fairly triumphant about his demeanour. After ten minutes someone else came rushing back with four typed copies of the undertaking and we both signed each copy, there was more shaking of hands and all seemed well.

We climbed back to our box where I was immediately asked if I would speak to two unintelligible Indians on the telephone, which was a less than instructive exercise. Next I was told to go to the front and put on headphones and to my astonishment I found myself talking to Telecom in London. I was told that the BBC did not want the line until 4.30 Indian time and so I asked if I could speak to Broadcasting House myself. That was impossible, so I asked the chap to relay a message back. Soon the answer came. The BBC were not taking commentary or live reports as the organisers had insisted on trying to extract more money even though the BBC had already bought the rights to broadcast the matches in which England were involved. There was no way they were going to pay any more.

This news put me on the spot, for I had just signed the BBC's life away. The Boil had gone down to the press box and so after telling all those within hearing that we would not be doing any live coverage. I raced back downstairs to Ranga Chara's office. I gave him the facts and without a word he led me out of his office past several security people into the office of Mr M.A. Chidambharam, the president of the Tamil Nadu Cricket Association, after whom the Chepauk Stadium had been recently named. He sat behind his desk in horn-rimmed glasses like a benevolent despot – the most friendly and charming of men. I explained the situation in something of a rush and apologised profusely and now it was his turn to say nothing. At once he opened the top left-hand drawer of his desk and took out a neatly folded piece of paper which turned out to be the top copy of our recent contract. He handed it to Ranga Chara who, with something of a flourish, tore up all four copies.

When the line eventually came through at 4.30 a thrilling finish was in progress. We took a chance and commentated on the last two balls of a match Australia won by one run when Maninder Singh was bowled by Steve Waugh with the last ball of the match.

I would have done the whole over but when Backers handed C.M-J. a note in Gujranwala telling him to hand over to HB in Madras, he unfortunately read it as 4B.

When it was all over, our pulse rates had subsided and we had finished our work, The Boil and I set off to find our taxi, leaving Alan Lee to join us when he had finished in the telex room. We walked on and on and could not find it in any of the

Sunil Gavaskar, who followed brilliance at Nagpur against New Zealand with a sad exit from cricket in the semi-final at Bombay. All-Sport/Adrian Murrell

140

car parks. In the end we gave up and returned to look for Alan, but he had already set out in search of us and we had lost each other. The Boil was not well – he had a bad stomach and was beginning to look as if he was on his last legs. By then, we had agreed that our best option was to walk in the other direction which led to a main street and pick up a taxi there.

On the way I remembered that I had a small flask of whisky in my briefcase. I asked The Boil if he had ever regarded me as a St Bernard dog. He looked puzzled and then I handed him the flask. He seized upon it gratefully and within two minutes was like a new man. When we reached the main road I hailed an auto-rickshaw and, sitting side by side, we were driven back to the Connemara Hotel, looking for all the world like Dr Livingstone and friend. The non-appearance of the taxi was a severe knock for Bailey Travel. One way and another it had been quite a day.

The five weeks in India have left me with a kaleidoscope of memories and if the vagaries of transport are high on my list it is because Indian taxi and rickshaw drivers have a habit of fitting a year's excitement into a two-mile journey. Red lights, double white lines and pedestrian crossings are largely for decoration. Yet, having said that, India is the most fascinating of countries and I love it, however unpredictable it may be by western standards. The people are delightful; the food is delicious – I always come away spiced to the eyeballs – there is so much to see and a strong sense of history. But to enjoy India it is essential to adapt yourself to the much slower way of life. If you spend your time comparing everything by western standards you are sunk. The real horrors are those who spend their entire time on the sub-continent bawling out everyone from waiters to taxi drivers to telephone operators and so on.

H.B.

My next encounter with Blowers was in the West End Hotel, Bangalore. I was in a hurry and worried that there might not be time for breakfast. There was no problem because I simply ate Henry's eggs and bacon and repaid him with the loan of my room, as he was not only delicate, but was also claiming to be the only constipated man on the sub-continent.

The English memsahibs of Victorian and Edwardian times gained a well-deserved reputation for getting the impossible done in India and Greta provided another example. As a result of a slight error on my part, we arrived at Bangalore airport early in the morning to fly to Indore, after changing planes at Bombay, with tickets which were valid for the following day. Greta does not believe in giving up, so despite the fact that both aircraft were not only full, but had long lists of stand-by passengers, she talked her way on to both by a combination of bluff, low cunning and sheer determination which had me applauding wildly.

It was a pity that Blowers did not come to Indore, because I would have preferred him to have dealt with the minor problem of being told by Radio India on the ground that the BBC had a circuit at the end of the match, but it did not work. In situations like that he has a tendency to become rather cross, which is always enormous fun, especially when neither party really understands what the other is saying. Henry would also have enjoyed the tight security, which meant that one was liable to trip over police and guns coming out of one's bedroom. However, it would have taken more than the might of the Indian Security Forces to stop Greta taking her lighter into the ground, though they did try. A New Zealand girl was even prevented from bringing in oranges, for fear the players might think they were cricket balls.

Henry and I joined up again in Delhi for the India versus Australia game and the Taj Palace Hotel served as a general meeting place as the England, West Indian and Sri Lankan teams drifted in and out. In addition, the VIPs and the not-so-important persons from the Test nations of the world were on parade. At breakfast I encountered Peter May and Raman Subba Row, had a beer with Clive Lloyd and lunch with Donald Carr. Blowers and J.J. Warr came in for a few drinks in our bedroom and we dined with Mr and Mrs Peter Short from Barbados.

For me, one of the attractions of Chandigarh was that I had been booked in (or at least I thought I had been) to a hotel called the Sixer, which was owned by Kapil Dev. I simply could not resist the name. Although it subsequently transpired that I was not expected, I had no problem joining the other press. Matthew Engel of the *Guardian* took me to what turned out to be a remarkable and memorable rock garden when I was expecting a beer garden playing rock music. The catering facilities for the media at Chandigarh were the best I encountered throughout India. The general standard, with the exception of Bombay, was not only very good, but far better than expected. Henry breezed in a day after me, but naturally in time to attend an excellent dinner given by the Governor of the Punjab, surely the most demanding appointment in the land. Blowers and I did experience a little difficulty getting there, because Indian taxi drivers seldom seem to know where places are, in spite of the fact that the Governor's residence must have been about the best-known building in the town. Once there however, Henry was in his element, hardly drawing breath. I stayed behind for an extra night before setting off for Nagpur via Delhi and what turned out to be my worst journey, which took about 36 hours, instead of about four, but spontaneous Indian hospitality greatly helped.

Having discovered at the airport that there would be a three-hour delay, I was adopted by three Indians, who took me to Kapil Dev's hotel for a very good lunch in the Sixer bar. We returned to the airport to find that the plane had been delayed for a further three hours. I passed the time by visiting a tyre retread factory, which is big business out there, taking a healthy walk beside a man-made lake, and being entertained at home. On arrival in Delhi, I discovered there were no flights to Indore until the following afternoon and, with the aid of another Good Samaritan in the same predicament, eventually secured accommodation in an hotel from Indian Airways.

Nagpur may be the centre of India, but it is not the most beautiful place and the Radikha Hotel and its manager – these things do tend to go together – were the worst I encountered throughout my visit. However, both Blowers and I were pleased we went, as we had the privilege and the pleasure of witnessing a Gavaskar century of purity, power and precision. The 'little master' only played two slogs and perhaps three slightly false shots, otherwise it was an innings of absolute perfection and showed that it is still possible to score very fast against defensive bowling and fields with text-book strokes.

It was back to Bombay and the Taj Mahal hotel, which Blowers regards as his permanent residence in India. Enjoying the view of the bay from his balcony with a glass of whisky in one's hand it is easy to understand why. Here we joined the rest of the *Test Match Special* team, who had been in Pakistan to provide ball-by-ball commentary on the semi-final between India and England, made even more satisfactory by England's victory. This triumph owed everything to batting first, having lost the toss, and Graham Gooch's innings, in which he swept and lapped the two Indian spinners so effectively. His tactics upset the rhythm of both Maninder and Shastri and they failed to set the right field. It was a remarkable knock and his assessment of line and length was outstanding, but why India, with much the stronger batting line-up, should have prepared a very slow turner was decidedly odd.

Henry and I were again in action in Calcutta for the final between England and Australia which the Aussies won by seven runs. Although the match was close, it is asking a great deal of a team with only five batsmen to make over 250 runs batting second, a task which always looked just out of our reach. It would have taken a major innings from Gooch, Gatting or Lamb to have made sure that we never dropped too far behind the asking rate of just over five runs per over, but it was not forthcoming. The game was, of course, really lost in the first nine overs by the England new-ball pair DeFreitas and Small. On a pitch which gave them some initial assistance they not only were guilty of inaccuracy, but also committed the sin of being no-balled far too frequently. The outcome was that Australia reached 48 after only nine overs without having taken any chances, and, but for some fine containment by the other members of the attack, particularly Foster, they could well have finished with a much larger total.

Although it was sad for England not to win the World Cup, all credit was due to Australia, who were a very well-disciplined team, splendidly managed by Alan Crompton, coached by Bobby Simpson and controlled by Allan Border on the field. They were the best fielding side in the tournament and a team in every sense.

On the day following the final Blowers flew off to Australia to see Ian Botham play his first game for Queensland and I returned to London, but not without some minor mishaps, like losing my ticket in the airport. This did cause some problems for the Air India staff, who could not have been more helpful. They even provided me with cups of coffee until I found my ticket hiding in my handkerchief.

T.B.

The World Cup itself was, considering the potential problems, extremely well organised. The hotels in the big centres were excellent and in the smaller towns they were adequate in a rather fundamental Indian style which is, I suppose, one way of saying how spoilt we have all become. The grounds exceeded all expectations and for me the pride of place went to Eden Gardens, Calcutta, which surely has become the most impressive ground in the world, and Chandigarh, the home of Kapil Dev, where 25,000 turned up to watch Australia beat New Zealand. Chandigarh is also the home of the convener of the World Cup, Inderjit Singh Bindra, who was responsible for making the whole thing work so well in India. Nothing was too much trouble for him and his attention to detail was brilliant. He was undoubtedly one of

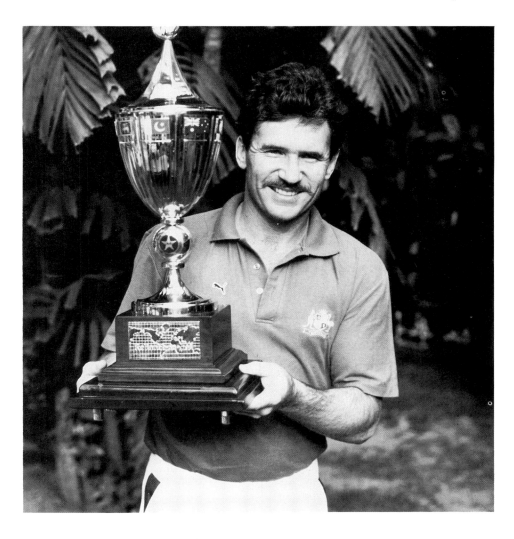

Allan Border proudly displays the 1987
World Cup.   Graham Morris

the heroes of the competition. He and his beautiful wife were also two of the most delightful companions for those of us who were lucky enough to get to know them.

The tournament produced some wonderful matches, too. The most exciting was Zimbabwe's failure by three runs to beat New Zealand at Hyderabad when David Houghton hit a remarkable 141, the most amazing one-day innings I have seen, after Zimbabwe, who needed 243, had lost their first seven wickets for 104. The two most perfect innings I watched were both played by Sunil Gavaskar in his last fling as an Indian cricketer. The first came in that opening match in Madras and although it produced only 37 runs it was devastating in its brilliance. The second, in Nagpur against New Zealand, brought him 103 not out, his first hundred in a one-day international. He played this innings, which was again technically perfect, on a very hot day with a fever and a temperature of more than 100 degrees. The determination of Gavaskar at such a late stage of his career was extraordinary. Maninder Singh's slow left-arm bowling was a delight, and Steve Waugh's accuracy in the closing overs was an object lesson, as was Craig McDermott's throughout. John Traicos's controlled off-spin, David Boon's ferocious stroke-play – marred only by his reluctance to leave the crease when given out – the Australian fielding and throwing and Martin Crowe's staggering catch running away from the wicket at long-on which ended Houghton's innings at Hyderabad are vibrant memories.

There were other moments, too. In Delhi one evening at the start of my tenth internal flight in India I found myself being charged overweight by a very grumpy official and soon afterwards I had a memorable chat with the airport manager. What was it I said about foreigners who shouted the odds in India? To my great embarrassment this particular discussion took place in front of The Boil. It was in some ways gratifying, therefore, to see or rather hear him trying to pay his hotel bill in Nagpur with a Visa card and then a Gold Visa card. The manager of the Radikha Hotel was not in the least impressed by either and The Boil's resulting baritone would have made Pavarotti look to his laurels.

In the press box at Chandigarh waiters with trays offered all and sundry frothing glasses of beer at 9.40 in the morning. It was certainly my earliest ever glass of beer on the sub-continent. At one point when we were about to pay our hotel bills (it may even have been on that famous occasion in Nagpur), after The Boil had been boasting about his prowess at packing, a bearer came downstairs clutching a dressing-gown which The Boil in his enthusiasm had forgotten to slip into his suitcase. I am glad to say that on the one occasion I saw the inside of his packed case I realised that I had at last met someone who is even less skilled than I am in this particular art.

The party in Chandigarh at the Governor of the Punjab's house was terrific. Sir Edmund Hillary of Everest fame was among those present and the lady Governor protested mildly when later in the evening I called her the Governess. I could go on like this forever, for they were five unforgettable weeks. My only worries concern the future of Bailey Travel.

H.B.

With England in Pakistan 1987

Peter Baxter,

When the England team returned to Pakistan on 12 November to start a six-week tour, it seemed to the accompanying media party that we would have a job to keep our readers and listeners interested after the World Cup extravaganza. Certainly Pakistan did not seem all that keen on the tour, an impression that was reinforced by the minute crowds and implied by the faded and torn posters that were the legacy of the World Cup. But it was a tour that was to rock the cricket world and to be compared with the 'bodyline' series for its impact.

We started in a sort of end-of-term atmosphere after the Calcutta final, arriving in Rawalpindi four days after that great occasion with the team and the press party both somewhat changed. Those of us who had witnessed England's eight World Cup matches were looking forward to a leisurely three-day game to start the Pakistan leg, but the one served up turned out to be a monumental bore. To be fair, it was used by several players to give themselves time in the middle after so much one-day cricket, Robinson and Athey each taking advantage of that chance by scoring a century. It was all rather irrelevant to the next phase, which was the series of three One-Day Internationals, to be played, after quite a bit of last-minute rearrangement, in widely separated cities over five days.

The last-minute nature of the rearranged matches meant that we had a few accommodation problems, principally for the first match in Lahore, previously scheduled for Hyderabad. The press hotel booked as the only one available by the Pakistan Cricket Board could most kindly be described as having 'character', and more realistically as being gloomy and grubby. The alternative offered by our travel agents was even more forbidding and its manager revealed that he had given away our rooms anyway.

The first One-Day International itself was played on a slow turning pitch, prepared, presumably, for Abdul Qadir, who had bowled so well in the World Cup. But Pakistan were themselves bowled out on it for 166, Emburey taking 3 for 17. Still Qadir had enough time to strike some terror into English hearts by removing Gooch and Gatting and we were given an introduction to some strange decisions by an umpire whose name was to become rather familiar – Shakoor Rana. In the end, though, England did get home by two wickets with three balls to spare.

Two days later and 650 miles south in Karachi in much warmer weather Graham Gooch batted for 43 of England's 44 overs to make 142, supported by David Capel towards the end with 50 not out, which included three successive sixes off Shoaib

Mohammed. Abdul Qadir was captaining the Pakistan side for these three matches because of the illness of the newly-appointed national captain, Javed Miandad, and here he had to call on no fewer than eight bowlers, he himself inevitably achieving the best figures of eight overs, 3 for 30. His team made a tremendous attempt on their target of six an over. Rameez Raja provided the backbone, being out off the last ball of the innings, 'obstructed the field' for 99 as he looked for the single which would have given him his hundred. Shoaib made 37, but it was while Salim Malik (35), Mansoor Elahi (17) and Ejaz Ahmed (26) were in with Rameez that England looked most in danger. They won the match eventually by 24 runs and thus made sure of the series. Still, the next morning we were on board an ancient patched-up 707 to fly to Peshawar, 700 miles to the north.

This frontier city had appealed to me when we were there for the World Cup. This time John Woodcock of *The Times* insisted on taking a small group of us to dinner at Dean's Hotel – *the* place to stay in Peshawar in days gone by and indeed where he had stayed on earlier tours, riding to the cricket on a horse-drawn tonga cart. Much of Dean's' old-fashioned comfort had gone now and was certainly not helped by faded decorations and a garishly-lit dining-room. The small bar, where once a chota peg might have slipped down all too easily after a day up in the hills, now had only a line of lemonade bottles in deference to the new Islamic masters.

The following day I had the first serious trouble I had met with the satellite circuits in Pakistan. It is inevitable on these occasions that you are told, 'There is no booking', but we made contact with London eventually on those non-existent circuits. Luckily, as it was a Sunday, my programme of reports was not as heavy as usual, so there was not too much harm done. England wrapped up the one-day series with their third win, making 236. Pakistan were never really in the hunt in the face of some hostile bowling by Foster and DeFreitas, although Salim Malik again threatened for a while. The Pakistan team left Peshawar in some haste that night by road for Islamabad and thence to Lahore for urgent consideration at high level on how this dangerous trend of English victory might be halted. England, as they awaited the next day's direct flight, had no illusions that these wins would make the task ahead in the Test series any easier.

It was a treat to arrive in a place where we could unpack for a full week's stay – something of a novelty on this tour. At last, too, we could turn our attention to a Test match. The same pitch used for the Lahore One-Day International awaited, clearly again left under-prepared for Abdul Qadir. Even Javed Miandad, now restored to health, admitted that it might take a bit of spin when I interviewed him on the eve of the match.

On the day he had three spinners in his side and only one specialist fast bowler, Wasim Akram. Abdul Qadir was bowling half-an-hour after the start, with the toss

Abdul Qadir, the genius who took 30
wickets in the three-match series.
Graham Morris

having been won by England. Throughout that early period *Test Match Special* was struggling every bit as much as England were to do later. The circuit failed to materialise, with the Pakistan telecom department at the satellite station in Karachi assuring my Pakistan Broadcasting Corporation engineers that there was – again – 'no booking'.

As the first over was being bowled, we did at last establish contact on the telephone with the studio in London. Our producer there, Joanne Watson, told me that they were in contact with Islamabad – the problems of having the luxury of two satellite stations to choose from were becoming apparent. While the engineers wrestled with that one, I started commentary on the telephone. This was situated in the corridor behind the commentary boxes. Fortunately the back walls of the commentary boxes were glazed, so that one could see the pitch, if not the whole outfield, through two sheets of glass. Unfortunately Pakistani glaziers do not often use Pilkington's finest and my view was somewhat distorted. To see the scoreboard I was looking at an angle through three panes and the distortion made it virtually impossible to read. By the end of half-an-hour when Jack Bannister, my co-commentator, relieved me my memory for the runs that had been scored was sorely stretched. Happily, 40 minutes into the day, we were broadcasting by more conventional means from our commentary point in front of the boxes on an open balcony – a choice in which the PBC had agreed to humour our eccentricity. Apart from Jack Bannister and myself, we had in the *TMS* team Mike Selvey, formerly of Middlesex, Glamorgan and England and now covering his first tour as cricket

Commentary by 'phone in Lahore. Jack Bannister waits to take over from   *co-commentator Peter Baxter.*
Graham Morris

correspondent of the *Guardian*, and Intikhab Alam, former captain of Pakistan and a great favourite in England from his days at Surrey. As the scorer previously arranged with the PBC failed to materialise we were very lucky to acquire the services of Jo King, the girlfriend of Ted Corbett of the *Star*. She did the job as to the manner born. With our problems off the field solved, things began to go sadly wrong for England on it. From being 22 for no wicket after 55 minutes, they were 94 for 8 halfway through the afternoon session and that only thanks to Chris Broad's watchful 41. To make matters worse, four of the dismissals had had a considerable element of doubt about them.

All but one of the wickets had fallen to Qadir, who was, despite the questionable umpiring, bowling brilliantly. That England got to 175 in the next couple of hours was thanks to spirited play by Foster who made 39, French (38 not out) and Cook, whose 10 was one of only five double-figure scores. Qadir had taken nine wickets for 56 and when I interviewed the maestro at the end of the day, when Pakistan were 13 for no wicket, he told me how painful his back was after 37 consecutive overs of leg-spin, googlies and flippers.

Pakistan batted throughout the second day, a day which for us on *TMS* was interrupted by infuriating and inexplicable line-breaks that often had Jack or me commentating from that same telephone with the restricted view. By the close the Pakistan lead was 102 and Mudassar had made 120, just by waiting for the bad balls to score off. On the third day England exerted more control until Wasim Akram and Abdul Qadir, with 40 and 38, took the match beyond their reach.

Thirty-five minutes before tea on the third day, England started their second innings 217 runs behind and by the close were 47 for 4 after yet more poor umpiring decisions and an unlovely incident in which Broad, who received probably the worst decision of the lot, stood his ground for about a minute before Gooch persuaded him to leave. Gooch was rewarded for his good sense by also being at the rough end of umpire Shakil Khan's lightning fickle finger.

Broad's histrionics at the crease had served to highlight an increasingly desperate position which had deepened to the point where the tour manager, Peter Lush, came to the press hotel that evening to make a statement, more in sorrow than in anger, in which he said, after condemning Broad's action, that a visiting team should at least be given the chance to compete on equal terms. The implication was clear that the poor umpiring decisions were not being regarded by the England team as simply incompetence, but as something much more sinister. It was a sad night for all those with the love of the game at heart and there was more than a suspicion that revenge was being taken for indignities, real or imagined, suffered during Pakistan's summer tour of England.

Two and a half hours into the fourth day it was all over and England had gone down to defeat by an innings and 87 runs, a defeat which was accompanied by bitter words from Mike Gatting and Micky Stewart. I feared for the state of mind of the England dressing-room, understandable as it was. After talking to my office in London, I feared, too, that hysteria was taking over at home. The time surely had come to cool things down. But the Pakistan Board showed little inclination to ease matters, handing Peter Lush a press release, already issued to the local newspapers, which stated that the umpires for the Second Test would be Khyzer Hyatt and Shakoor Rana.

After such a traumatic start to the series it was probably just as well that England's next fixture was a three-day match against the Punjab Chief Minister's XI in the country town of Sahiwal previously known as Montgomery, about 100 miles south-west of Lahore. The team, all but Gatting, Gooch, Foster and the manager, Peter Lush, who stayed in Lahore, were accommodated in the local biscuit factory, while the seven members of the media who made the trip were billetted in the government rest house. It was no luxury hotel, but comfortable enough and we were looked after by a serious-looking Punjabi named Fazal, whose smile, sparingly used, was a great reward when it came. By happy chance, among our select group was Qamar Ahmed, Reuters' man on the tour, who included Punjabi in his extensive linguistic repertoire. For the three nights that we were there the entertainment included carpet cricket with golf ball, clothes brush and a few bleeding knuckles, and carpet bowls with golf ball woods and a cricket ball donated by Micky Stewart as the jack.

Telephone calls out of Sahiwal were a problem, but I discovered in the town on the first evening an evil little telegraph office which resembled a Victorian coal-hole where the official, sitting on a tall stool with a large ledger in front of him, got me through to London in one minute flat. Thereafter things became much easier, with London able to ring me at the ground.

On the field Robinson made 51, Athey 43 and French 45 in a total of 279 to which the Chief Minister's XI replied with 215. England used the last day largely for batting practice, eventually declaring at 222 for 5 thanks to 76 from Robinson and 66 from Fairbrother. A few wry smiles were raised by the appearance of Pakistan's chief selector, Haseeb Ahsan. The young leg-spinner, Mushtaq Ahmed, who had taken six wickets in the first innings was suddenly removed from the attack in the second innings. English inexperience at playing leg-spin must, after all, be preserved. We were reminded of occasions when leg-spinners expected for net sessions had mysteriously not appeared.

In the last half-hour Dilley and DeFreitas had time to cause some alarm among the opposition before the match was called off as a draw and we boarded our small coaches for the three-hour drive through the agricultural plain of the Punjab to Faisalabad. It was a nightmarish journey in the dark, frequently behind overladen donkey carts and along roads whose surface would disappear without warning. The brand new hotel in Faisalabad was a haven of rest and comfort when we reached it. Little did we know of the troubles that lay ahead.

The Iqbal Stadium pitch 48 hours before the Test match had the look of another raging turner. When I stood on it to interview Micky Stewart it was cracked and crumbling and the groundsman assured us that it would get no more water before the match. The next morning it had bound together much more. He must have watered it within an hour of telling us he would not. Could it have been, I wondered, that he had heard of Abdul Qadir's back pains?

The Pakistan selectors, however, decided to pin their faith on their spinners again, and did not include a single specialist seam bowler in their side. They opened their attack, when England won the toss, with Mudassar and the new cap, Aamir Malik, who was there primarily as a batsman. In fact his main role turned out to be as a silly mid-off, in which position he took the first two catches – Gooch and Athey – apparently off the pad, after the spinners had come on in the eighth over. England's approach was positive, though, particularly when Gatting came in to play a magnificently belligerent innings which brought him 79 from 81 balls with 14 fours. The third wicket stand of 117 with Broad was assembled at a run a minute, so the loss of Gatting, bowled cutting at Qadir's flipper, was a blow. Robinson was another Qadir victim before the close, but I was delighted to be on the air when Chris Broad reached his century in the penultimate over of the first day.

Before the second day was over we were to witness an incident which would cause a rumpus to chase all but the Reagan-Gorbachev summit off the front pages of the newspapers. But for much of the day we were able to enjoy the prospect of a very good Test match in the making. England had been rapidly dismissed in the morning for 292 and then had struck back, taking the first five Pakistan wickets for 77. As Ejaz Ahmed was one of them, even the incident when Shakoor Rana refused to give him out for an apparent catch off a glove at short leg could be ignored.

In what was possibly the last over of the day, although England were pressing to get another in, Pakistan had reached 105 for 5. I was commentating with Intikhab as Eddie Hemmings ran in from the pavilion end to bowl to Salim Malik. The ball was delivered, but suddenly we were aware of an extraordinary shouting match between Gatting, who was at short leg, and the square leg umpire, Shakoor Rana. There was a great deal of pointing and, although the other umpire, Khyzer Hyatt, at the bowler's end signalled 'dead ball' in view of the rumpus, we had no immediate idea what it was about. It did, however, look a thoroughly undignified scene.

Back at the hotel some of the details started to leak out. Shakoor had apparently shouted at Gatting to stop moving the field as the bowler was coming in. Of his initial address to the England captain only the word 'cheat' was broadcastable. Gatting had, not surprisingly, responded in similar vein. Although they went on to finish that over and the day's play with it, later that night we heard that Shakoor Rana had refused to stand in the match next day unless he received an apology from Mike Gatting for the language used to him.

Next morning Mike led his team on to the field on the dot at 10.00 a.m., the official starting-time, although the stumps were not set and the groundstaff were still in the middle with the stationary roller and mower. No umpires appeared, nor did the Pakistan batsmen. Meetings started in the offices of the pavilion and after half-an-hour the players drifted back to the dressing-room. Mike Gatting, we heard, was prepared to offer an apology, but wanted one from Shakoor Rana in return. That the umpire was not prepared to give. From early optimism the crisis deepened into a

deadlock with an apparent lack of will by the Pakistan Cricket Board officials to sort things out. While Peter Lush and Micky Stewart were back at the hotel contacting Lord's by telephone, the Board secretary, Ejaz Butt, left without a word to them for Lahore. So Lush did the same, to try to see the Board president, Lt General Safdar Butt, who had not been available to speak to him by telephone all day.

Not a ball was bowled on that third day which ended without an apparent solution in sight. On *Test Match Special* we had opened up on time and had talked our way through the day with considerable help from the presenter in London, David Mercer, who brought an interesting angle from his time as a tennis umpire, and from Christopher Martin-Jenkins, who was having to rush all over Broadcasting House doing comment pieces. For this Test we had acquired the services of Ralph Dellor, who had come out to see the last two Tests and found life much more eventful than he had anticipated. He did powerful and athletic work up and down the stairs. Joanne Watson had also found a great deal of standby material to give us – and the listeners – a break from time to time. That night we heard from Lahore that – incredibly – General Butt had been out when Peter Lush tried to see him. It was difficult to regard this as anything other than a deliberate snub.

The official rest day which followed was anything but that for the press party. Developments were slow and few and there was much hanging around the hotel foyer and coffee shop and in my case, my room, by the telephone on which I reported during the day for Radios 4, 2, 1, World Service and BBC Television. Encouraging statements were issued by the Pakistan Cricket Board in Lahore, but Peter Lush was grim-faced when he returned to Faisalabad that afternoon, and he said that no real progress had been made. And none was that day, although we awaited developments into the small hours of the morning.

The break came next morning. As on every Friday, the scheduled start was earlier, to cope with the Muslim sabbath's extended lunch interval, but the team arrived at the ground later than usual, having had a meeting before leaving the hotel. They had another at the ground at which they were told that there was no move from Shakoor Rana and so Gatting, ordered to do so by the Test and County Cricket Board, was signing an apology. The players made it clear that they were still fully behind their captain, but Shakoor had his scrap of paper, which he brandished for anyone who wanted to see it. It was a fairly perfunctory apology, written in capitals:

DEAR SHAKOOR RANA
I APOLOGISE FOR THE BAD LANGUAGE
USED DURING THE 2nd DAY OF THE TEST
MATCH AT FISALABAD (sic)
And it was signed, Mike Gatting.

Confrontation at Faisalabad: Mike Gatting
and Shakoor Rana.   Graham Morris

Peter Baxter, able at last to enjoy cricket in
Faisalabad.   Peter Baxter

The match re-started after a 25-minute delay, but it was a day thoroughly in tune with the sorry situation. For once it was cold and grey and there was the occasional spit of rain. After 15 minutes the players were off again and although the light improved a lot it became clear that, with Pakistan not in the healthiest of positions, the officials had no great interest in getting the game going.

'We are waiting for the sun,' said the umpires when the photographers showed them their light meters. That sun did eventually emerge, killing any further excuses, and we had two hours' play in which Neil Foster vented his fury and Pakistan were dismissed for 191 – 101 runs behind, but with only one day to go.

At the close of play the players issued their own statement on the affair which had held up the Test match and the climb-down which had re-started it:

'The England players deplore the fact that it was not possible to effect a compromise between Mike Gatting and Shakoor Rana. We would have expected the governing bodies of both countries to use their influence and authority to resolve the problem.

What is beyond dispute is that the umpire was the first to use foul and abusive language to the England captain. This was clearly heard by the England players

156

close to the incident. Mike Gatting was ready to apologise two days ago for his response, provided the umpire would do the same.

We also wish to register a unanimous protest that the TCCB should consider it necessary to issue instructions through our manager, Peter Lush, to order the captain to make an unconditional apology to the umpire. By doing so, the captain in the "wider interests of the game" felt that he was forced to act against his own free will.

The Board exerted pressure on Mike Gatting and on the rest of us and we are unanimous in the view that the same "wider interests of the game" referred to by our Board had been completely ignored by the Pakistan Board, who did not exert similar pressure on the umpire.

The incident was sad for cricket, but the solution forced upon us is even sadder.'

There were few, if any, among the press there who did not have considerable sympathy with the team.

Graham Gooch tried hard to put something into the final day of the Test with a splendid 65 off only 74 balls, but apart from Athey's 20 no one else really got going and the declaration in mid-afternoon asking Pakistan to score 239 in probably 40 overs was not answered. Uniquely, in my experience, Miandad felt empowered to offer Gatting the chance to call it off before the last 20 overs had started. Another example of the idiosyncrasies of the East.

We had looked ahead a month before and earmarked the three days in Karachi before the final Test as a chance to top up suntans and do our Christmas shopping in the Bazaar, but after the events of Faisalabad, they were tense days when at times it was not certain that the match would be played or that, if it was, Mike Gatting would lead England out in it. Raman Subba Row and Alan Smith, chairman and chief executive respectively of the Test and County Cricket Board, arrived 48 hours before the match for a day of meetings with the management and the players. When they emerged to face the press, they looked fairly shaken by the strength of feeling they had encountered and were similarly surprised to find the press of a like mind. It was clear that they had modified their view from the one formed 6,000 miles away at Lord's.

The other saga which ran through the build-up to the match was yet again the umpires. It became clear, although it was never officially admitted, that the name of Shakil Khan, the man responsible for the trouble in the First Test, had been put forward in what could only have been a mischievous move. The Pakistan Board then went through a pantomime of offering to bring in umpires from another country, a scheme which even if it had been handled efficiently would probably have failed from lack of time. But at last they named umpire Mahboob Shah, considered their best, who had stood in the World Cup final, and Khyzer Hyatt.

On Wednesday 16 December England won the toss and for the third time in the series batted first. Fifty minutes after lunch they seemed doomed to defeat at 85 for

6 – three wickets to Qadir after Wasim Akram's initial breakthrough. But Capel and Emburey put on 114 for the seventh wicket, and although Emburey went for 70 in the last half-hour, French showed every sign of carrying on the good work. He was out to the last ball before lunch on the second day for 31, and Capel was last out for 98, richly deserving to have scored those two runs for his maiden Test hundred.

In reply a second-wicket stand between Rameez Raja and Salim Malik seemed to be taking the game away from England but three quick wickets before the close put Pakistan back on their heels. It was turning out to be a fine Test match, showing what could be done when both sides had faith in the integrity of the umpires. And it was greatly enjoyed by our new summariser, Robin Marlar, who was to be with us for the first three days in place of the Lahore-based Intikhab. Robin's place was taken for the last two days by Sadiq Mohammed of Gloucestershire and Pakistan, whose great trick was to pick Qadir's googlies from the hand as he was commentating.

Two more early wickets on the third morning gave England genuine hopes of a surprise last-ditch win. But Wasim Akram and Abdul Qadir again showed what tremendous value they are to Pakistan with their lower-order batting, Qadir hitting Emburey, who was otherwise a model of economy, for four straight sixes. Both those two batsmen stole the limelight, while they were in, from a remarkable innings by Aamir Malik. At times he looked frightful and at others completely strokeless, but then he would cut loose with devastating effect. He ran out of partners at 98, by which time David Capel had taken his first Test wicket, clean bowling Qadir for 61 with his first ball in the match. By that time, too, it was the fourth morning. Pakistan had a lead of 59 and time was running out for England.

Time could not run out fast enough for them when the fourth wicket went down when they were only two runs ahead. Salim Jaffer was now bowling splendidly as Qadir's foil. But at 115 for 5 those two inseparable friends, Graham Gooch and John Emburey, were united in a partnership which gradually began the saving of the match. It looked anything but saved when Gooch's wicket went to the unexpected agency of Mudassar with the new ball, followed quickly by French and DeFreitas on the final morning, but Nick Cook stayed manfully with Emburey in a ninth-wicket stand of 59 which ensured England's safety.

Abdul Qadir's five wickets in each innings had taken his tally to 30 for the three-match series. He was the difference between the two sides – too good a bowler to have the gilt taken off his gingerbread by the wiles of those who could not be content merely to rely on his skills. In this last Test the Pakistan Board had won a few more propaganda points, for their own consumption at any rate, and England had certainly helped in this by the revelation that the TCCB was awarding the England players a hardship bonus of £1,000 a man. Many of those who had sympathised with them winced at that.

On the last evening as we packed came the last 'sensation' of the tour. Javed Miandad was considering resigning the Pakistan captaincy. But by that time none of us cared. We were going home for Christmas.

SUMMARISED SCORES

First One-Day International at Lahore
Pakistan   166 (41.3 overs) (Emburey 3-17)
England   167 for 8 (44.3 overs) (Gooch 43; Wasim Akram 3-25)

Second One-Day International at Karachi
England   263 for 6 (Gooch 142; Capel 50 n o; Qadir 3-30)
Pakistan   240 for 8 (Rameez Raja 99)

Third One-Day International at Peshawar
England   236 for 8 (Broad 66; Gooch 57; Gatting 53; Qadir 3-49)
Pakistan   138 (Salim Malik 52; Foster 3-20)

First Test at Lahore: Pakistan won by an innings and 87 runs
England   175 (Broad 41; Quadir 9-56)
and   130 (Emburey 38 n o; Qadir 4-45)
Pakistan   392 (Mudassar 120; Miandad 65)

Second Test at Faisalabad: Drawn
England   292 (Broad 116; Gatting 79; Iqbal Qasim 5-83; Qadir 4-105)
and   137 for 6 dec. (Gooch 65)
Pakistan   191 (Salim Malik 60; Foster 4-42)
and   51 for 1

Third Test at Karachi: Drawn
England   294 (Capel 98; Emburey 31; Qadir 5-88)
and   268 for 9 (Gooch 93; Emburey 74 n o; Quadir 5-98)
Pakistan   353 (Aamir Malik 98 n o; Qadir 61; DeFreitas 5-86)